COMMUNICATING THE WORD

Communicating the Word

Revelation, Translation, and Interpretation in Christianity and Islam

A record of the seventh Building Bridges seminar
Convened by the Archbishop of Canterbury
Rome, May 2008

DAVID MARSHALL, EDITOR

GEORGETOWN UNIVERSITY PRESS
Washington, DC

Library of Congress Cataloging-in-Publication Data

Communicating the word : revelation, translation, and interpretation in Christianity and Islam : a record of the seventh Building Bridges seminar convened by the Archbishop of Canterbury, Rome, May 2008 / David Marshall, editor.
   p.   cm.
  Includes bibliographical references and index.
  ISBN 978-1-58901-784-9 (pbk. : alk. paper)
  1. Islam—Relations—Christianity—Congresses.   2. Christianity and other religions—Islam—Congresses.   3. Revelation—Islam—Congresses.
4. Revelation—Christianity—Congresses.   5. Koran—Criticism, interpretation, etc.—Congresses.   6. Bible—Criticism, interpretation, etc.—Congresses.
I. Marshall, David.
  BP172.C537   2011
  261.2'7—dc22
                                                                2011006189

15 14 13 12 11   9 8 7 6 5 4 3 2 First printing

Printed in the United States of America

Contents

Part III: Methods and Authority in Interpretation

Participants

Muhammad Abdel Haleem
King Fahd Professor of Islamic Studies, School of Oriental and African Studies, University of London

Amin Abdullah
Rector, State Islamic University (Universitas Islam Negeri), Yogyakarta, Indonesia

Asma Afsaruddin
Associate Professor of Arabic and Islamic Studies, Department of Classics, University of Notre Dame, Indiana

Seyed Amir Akrami
Lecturer, al-Mahdi Institute, Birmingham, UK

John Azumah
Senior Research Fellow, Akrofi-Christaller Memorial Centre, Akropong-Akuapem, Ghana

Osman Bakar
Professor of Islamic Thought and Civilization, International Institute of Islamic Thought and Civilization (ISTAC), Kuala Lumpur

Ellen F. Davis
Amos Ragan Kearns Distinguished Professor of Bible and Practical Theology, Duke University, Durham, North Carolina

Susan Eastman
Assistant Professor of the Practice of Bible and Christian Formation, Duke University, Durham, North Carolina

Michael Ipgrave
Archdeacon of Southwark, Church of England

John Langan
Rose Kennedy Professor of Christian Ethics, Georgetown University, Washington, DC

Daniel A. Madigan
Director of Graduate Studies, Department of Theology, Georgetown University, Washington, DC

Jane Dammen McAuliffe
President, Bryn Mawr College, Pennsylvania

Sohail Nakhooda
Editor-in-Chief, *Islamica* Magazine

Ng Kam Weng
Research Director, Kairos Research Centre, Kuala Lumpur

Mehmet Pacaci
Ankara University, Turkey

Abdullah Saeed
Director of Asia Institute, University of Melbourne, Australia

Lamin Sanneh
D. Willis James Professor of Missions & World Christianity and Professor of History, Yale University Divinity School, New Haven, Connecticut

Recep Şentürk
Professor of Sociology, Centre for Islamic Studies, Istanbul

Reza Shah-Kazemi
The Institute of Ismaili Studies, London

Mona Siddiqui
Professor of Islamic Studies and Public Understanding, University of Glasgow, UK

Rowan Williams
Archbishop of Canterbury, Church of England

Timothy Wright
Abbot Emeritus of Ampleforth Abbey, UK, and Adviser to the Abbot Primate on Benedictine-Muslim Relations

Acknowledgments

M any thanks are once again due to John J. DeGioia, president of George-town University, for generous support of the seventh Building Bridges seminar in Rome and also of the publication of this record of that seminar. Thanks also to Richard Brown and the staff of Georgetown University Press for their commitment to the Building Bridges process. It is a pleasure to work with them.

Introduction

DAVID MARSHALL

Beginning in January 2002, the series of Building Bridges seminars, convened and chaired by the Archbishop of Canterbury, has covered a wide range of themes at the heart of Muslim-Christian dialogue. This book offers a record of the seventh seminar, held from May 6–8, 2008, at Villa Palazzola, near Rome, formerly a Cistercian monastery and now owned by the Venerable English College. Whereas all previous seminars had included a public dimension, with lectures open to the public as well as closed sessions attended just by seminar participants, this seminar happened entirely in private. While this provided an ideal environment for twenty-two Christian and Muslim scholars to engage in open and far-reaching dialogue, it is all the more important that through this publication some account of the seminar's proceedings should be made more widely available.

The seminar focused on three themes: revelation, translation, and interpretation. Each of these themes was explored through both a pair of lectures and the study alongside each other of relevant Christian and Muslim texts (mainly scriptural) that had been chosen before the seminar in consultation with a number of participants. Following normal Building Bridges practice, a large amount of time was dedicated to discussion of these texts in groups of about seven members each. Before the group discussions a brief introduction was given to the texts in question. This book reproduces the lectures and the introductions to the selected texts, together with the texts themselves. No attempt is made to give a detailed record of the group discussions, although toward the end of the volume (in "Conversations in Rome") there is an account of the main themes of these discussions and also of the seminar's plenary sessions.

In part I ("Particularity, Universality, and Finality in Revelation"), Seyed Amir Akrami, referring to a wide range of Qur'ānic texts, addresses the relationship between the particularity of Islam as a specific religious tradition and the universality of *islām*, by which he means "the essential core of beliefs, attitudes and behaviors" underlying Islam and other religious traditions. His conclusion is that there is no contradiction in the Qur'ān's affirmation of both the particularity of Islam and the universality of *islām*. Daniel Madigan identifies four textual "hooks" in John's Gospel on which to hang reflections on creation, the particularity of the incarnation, the finality especially associated with the cross, and the coming of the Spirit to guide believers into all truth, noting that, as that process of guidance is ongoing, "finality is begun, but not yet finished." Madigan concludes that the particularities of the two faiths are what make us what we are "and who we are is where dialogue begins."

In both the Bible and the Qur'ān the ultimate revelation, whether seen as coming in Christ or in the Qur'ān itself, does not arrive without a prehistory of revelation. The first two sets of scriptural texts in part I (1.3 and 1.4) therefore focus on Israel. The biblical texts are concerned with both the particularity and the wider significance of Israel, its election, and its task among the nations. The Qur'ānic texts look back to revelation before Muhammad and the Qur'ān, focusing on Israel as a particular locus of earlier revelation. The texts in 1.5 illustrate how the New Testament conveys both the particularity and the universal significance of the revelation in Christ; these are followed by texts in 1.6 in which the Qur'ān speaks of itself and its revelation through Muhammad.

Here the question might be raised: what of revelation through nature, a theme in both the Bible and the Qur'ān? That theme was not tackled, both because it had been addressed in an earlier Building Bridges seminar[1] and also because the concern at this seminar was with how Christians and Muslims understand divine revelation as it has occurred at particular moments in history, rather than with continuous revelation through nature.

A question for each faith has been how to make its scripture understood in a linguistically plural world. The challenge sits differently in each faith, however, because for Christians scripture is generally understood as witnessing to the primary revelation in Christ, whereas for Muslims scripture is in itself the primary revelation. In part II ("Translating the Word?"), Muhammad Abdel Haleem explores Muslim attitudes to translating the Qur'ān. While he argues that the Qur'ān's own emphasis on the fact that it is in Arabic was not intended to discourage translation for the purposes of communication, he also stresses that for Muslims the Qur'ān is ultimately untranslatable because of the awe they feel toward its inimitable language. He also notes the centrality of the Arabic of the Qur'ān in Islamic worship and the powerfully unifying influence this has among all Muslims. In contrast, Lamin Sanneh argues that the impulse toward making scripture available in the vernacular is deeply embedded in the Christian faith. With particular reference to the translation of the King James Bible, he gives examples of the often heroic and sacrificial work of translators, for whom "The whole enterprise of translation seemed like fitting testimony to the God who knew the way of Calvary, and an instructive metaphor of the incarnation."

The different instincts within Christianity and Islam toward translating scripture are reflected in the very different kinds of texts discussed in part II. If there seems little connection between these biblical and Qur'ānic texts, this may point precisely to a significant asymmetry to be patiently and intelligently explored. The Qur'ānic texts in 2.4 focus on the fact that the Qur'ān is an Arabic scripture. This emphasis can be interpreted in terms of the need of the Qur'ān's immediate addressees to understand its message, but it is clearly also a factor in the traditional Islamic understanding of the untranslatability of the Qur'ān: it only is the Qur'ān in the original Arabic. In 2.6 we consider passages which in different ways suggest the exclusively divine origins of the Qur'ān, denying any human role in its composition. The biblical texts in 2.3 are concerned with quite different questions. Because in Christian perspective the ultimate revelation of the eternal divine Word is understood as being in the human life of Jesus, the question of the translation of the divine Word is not in the first place about scriptural translation. The Word that was made flesh in Jesus is further mediated through the church as the "Body of Christ" and in the Eucharistic presence of Christ's body and blood. In 2.5 we move on to the question: what, then, of scripture? How does it fit within an understanding of revelation at the heart of which is the incarnation? The biblical passages here are something of a collage of different sorts of texts variously suggesting the divine and/or human origins of scripture.

The outgoing impulse toward the communication of divine revelation is at work across cultures and the passage of time. It thus constantly encounters challenges calling for thought on how the revelation is to be interpreted in new contexts. This raises questions of method and authority. What are valid ways of interpretation, and who says? In part III ("Methods and Authority in Interpretation") these questions are addressed in the historical surveys presented by John Langan and Abdullah Saeed. Chapter 3.3 looks at Gospel texts that present Christ interpreting scripture in two different contexts, while 3.4 focuses on texts that have been significant in the history of the interpretation of the Qur'ān. Finally, in 3.5 and 3.6 we move beyond scripture to consider a pair of recently published texts concerned with the same broad theme. The selection of passages from *Generous Love* illustrates the use of scripture in a contemporary Anglican approach to relations with people of other faiths, while the final section of *A Common Word* discusses Qur'ānic texts relevant to relations with Christians.

Two final pieces seek to draw together some of the many strands in the discussions that took place over the three days of the seminar: "Conversations in Rome" presents an overview of some of the main themes that occurred in group discussions and plenary sessions and, in the Afterword, Rowan Williams offers his concluding reflections.

Note on Translations of the Bible and the Qur'ān

When not indicated otherwise in the notes, the translations of the Qur'ān in this volume are either from *The Qur'an: A New Translation,* M. A. S. Abdel Haleem (Oxford: Oxford University Press, 2004) or are the author's own translation. Translations of the Bible are either from the New Revised Standard Version or are the author's own translation.

Note

1. See Michael Ipgrave, ed., *Scriptures in Dialogue: Christians and Muslims Studying the Bible and the Qur'ān Together* (London: Church House, 2004), 43–50.

PART I

Particularity, Universality, and Finality in Revelation

1.1 Particularity and Universality in the Qur'ān

SEYED AMIR AKRAMI

The specific question I address here is whether Islam, as a particular religion arising in seventh-century Arabia with all its particular doctrines, ethics, laws, rituals, and various other aspects, is conceived by its revelatory source, namely the Qur'ān, to be applicable to and binding on all humanity, or whether it is thought to be the necessary way of attaining salvation and truth only for its own adherents. In other words, does the Qur'ān regard Islam as the only religion that provides universal access to ultimate happiness, or does it recognize other religions as salvific and hence religiously and spiritually effective for their followers?

The view I advocate is that the Qur'ān makes a clear distinction between, on the one hand, a universal, minimal, and essential core of beliefs, attitudes, and behaviors that it calls *islām*, and, on the other, the historical manifestations of *islām* in various times and places in the form of particular religions such as Judaism, Christianity, and Islam. In Qur'ānic terminology we can talk about this distinction in terms of the difference between *dīn*, which refers to the essential and universal set of beliefs and practices, and *sharī'a, shir'a,* and *manhaj*, which refer to the particular historical and institutionalized religions.[1] The universality lies in those fundamental attitudes and views, *islām*, rather than in a historical manifestation of it, namely Islam.

The first important point striking any reader of the Qur'ān in the context of religious diversity is its recurrent and overriding emphasis on a long and universal chain of revelation and prophecy in which Muhammad is only one link. This general stream of revelation, which can be identified with *islām*, includes all the prophets from Adam to Muhammad: "some [messengers] We have mentioned to you and some We have not" (Qur'ān 40:78; see also 3:144; 4:163–65; 10:47; 13:7; 16:36). In fact, "every community has been sent a warner" (35:24). This central Qur'ānic idea is highlighted in the following passage: "In matters

3

of faith, He has laid down for you [people] the same commandment that He gave Noah, which We have revealed to you [Muhammad] and which We enjoined on Abraham and Moses and Jesus: 'Uphold the faith and do not divide into factions within it'" (42:13).

The Qur'ān calls this religion or faith *islām* and therefore also explicitly describes the disciples of Abraham, Jacob, and Jesus as *"muslim"* (2:128, 132; 3:52; 5:111). The fact that the Qur'ān incorporates narratives about the lives of prophets before Muhammad strongly indicates its emphasis on the oneness of religion and the unity of the essential message of the different religious traditions, which took various historical forms relative to their differing situations and circumstances.

The Qur'ān stresses that Muhammad is "not told anything that the previous messengers were not told" (41:43). He is also instructed to say "I am not the first of God's messengers. I do not know what will be done with me or you; I only follow what is revealed to me; I only warn plainly" (46:9). In this context Muslims are warned not to think of themselves as the privileged or distinguished people of God and if they turn back (from the path of *islām*) "He will substitute other people for you if you turn away, and they will not be like you" (47:38).

Throughout the Qur'ān there is a special and significant emphasis on this general revelatory phenomenon, to which Muslims are told to give verbal recognition: "So [you believers], say, 'We believe in God and in what was sent down to us and what was sent down to Abraham, Ishmael, Isaac, Jacob, and the Tribes, and what was given to Moses, Jesus, and all the prophets by their Lord. We make no distinction between any of them, and we devote ourselves to Him" (2:136; see also 2:285; 3:84). This universal revelatory phenomenon, which I shall argue is called *islām* by the Qur'ān, is usually identified with the faith of Abraham (2:127–32).

The general Qur'ānic perspective is that this universal phenomenon of revelation has given rise to different historical forms of religiosity and that, as long as the adherents of these religions faithfully practice the essential elements of that Abrahamic heritage, their salvation is guaranteed. Therefore, if the Qur'ān sometimes denounces Christians and Jews it must be interpreted as referring to particular groups who did not act according to the main teachings of these religions, rather than to these traditions and their followers in their totality. Consideration of the Qur'ānic verses in which adherents of these religions are either praised or criticized clearly substantiates this view. Particular attention will be paid here to comments on these passages by Muhammad Husayn Tabataba'i (1903–82), a great Iranian scholar of Islamic philosophy, mysticism, and jurisprudence, and the author of a twenty-volume commentary on the Qur'ān in Arabic.

Among positive references to Christians we can cite the following: "There are people of the Book who, if you [Prophet] entrust them with a heap of gold, will return it to you intact, but there are others of them who, if you entrust them with a single dinar, will not return it to you unless you keep standing over them, because they say, 'We are under no obligation towards the gentiles'—they tell a lie against God and they know it. No indeed! God loves those who keep their pledges and are mindful of Him" (3:75–76). What is important here is the emphasis on the noble moral attitude of trustworthiness that makes some Christians praiseworthy and causes them to be described as mindful of God ("*muttaqī*" or displaying "*taqwā*," often translated "godfearing"). Tabataba'i comments that the purpose of this verse is that the nobility given by God is not something cheap that can be achieved easily so that anyone with any alleged relationship with God or ascription to any race can claim it. It is rather obtained through loyalty to God and His covenant and mindfulness of Him.[2]

A similar positive reference states: "But they are not all alike. There are some among the People of the Book who are upright, who recite God's revelations during the night, who bow down in worship, who believe in God and the Last Day, who order what is right and forbid what is wrong, who are quick to do good deeds. These people are among the righteous and they will not be denied [the reward] for whatever good deeds they do: God knows exactly who is conscious of Him" (3:113–15). Tabataba'i comments that in this passage the most important characteristics of righteousness, which are belief in God and the Last Day, commanding what is right and forbidding what is wrong, and competing in good acts, are attributed to these members of the People of the Book; they are therefore on the straight path. Although Tabataba'i mentions that it is said by earlier commentators that those who are praised here are a specific group (Abdullah ibn Salaam and his companions), I believe that he neither approves nor disapproves of leaving the verse open to a more inclusive interpretation.[3]

Again from the same sūra we read: "Some of the People of the Book believe in God, in what has been sent down to you and in what was sent down to them: humbling themselves before God, they would never sell God's revelation for a small price. These people will have their rewards with their Lord: God is swift in reckoning" (3:199). Again, qualities such as belief in God and revelations, humility before God, and steadfastness are very clearly ascribed to a group of the People of the Book. Tabataba'i's understanding of the text is that they will be rewarded with the believers, usually taken to refer to Muslims. He emphasizes that ultimate happiness in the hereafter is not the exclusive preserve of any particular group, so that the People of the Book would be precluded from it. Rather, the criterion is belief in God and His messengers and if the People of the Book meet that criterion they are on an equal footing with Muslims.[4]

Another relevant verse runs as follows: "We sent other messengers to follow in their footsteps. After those We sent Jesus, son of Mary: We gave him the Gospel and put compassion and mercy into the hearts of his followers. But monasticism was something they invented—We did not ordain it for them, only that they should seek God's pleasure—and even so, they did not observe it properly. So We gave a reward to those of them who believed, but many of them broke the rules" (57:27). Here once again positive moral qualities and spiritual practices are attributed to some followers of Jesus, particularly compassion, mercy, and monasticism, though there is also a critical reference to excess in observation of the monastic life. But the important point is that at the end faith or belief, central to *islām*, is ascribed to them. Tabataba'i's commentary here is general and brief, mostly concentrating on what monasticism means, but he closes his discussion by stating that "among them are believers rewarded for their faith, but many of them are transgressors."[5]

Christians are also praised in the following verses:

You [Prophet] are sure to find that the most hostile to the believers are the Jews and those who associate other deities with God; you are sure to find that the closest in affection toward the believers are those who say, "We are Christians," for there are among them people devoted to learning and ascetics. These people are not given to arrogance, and when they listen to what has been sent down to the Messenger, you will see their eyes overflowing with tears because they recognize the truth [in it]. They say, "Our Lord, we believe, so count us amongst the witnesses. Why should we not believe in God and in the truth that has come down to us when we long for our Lord to include us in the company of the righteous?" For saying this, God has rewarded them with Gardens graced with flowing streams, and there they will stay: that is the reward of those who do good (5:82–85).

The main reasons for this positive description are the presence of priests and monks, their humility and recognition of the truth, which make them eligible to be regarded as believers, righteous and worthy of God's reward and paradise. Tabataba'i here just paraphrases these qualities, emphasizing that among the Christians are learned men who remind their community of truth by word, and ascetics who remind them of the greatness of their Lord both by deed and also by their humble acceptance of the truth.[6]

Again, we read: "Those to whom We gave the Scripture before believe in it, and, when it is recited to them, say, 'We believe in it, it is the truth from our Lord. Before it came we had already devoted ourselves to Him.' They will be given their rewards twice over because they are steadfast, repel evil with good, give to others out of what We have provided for them, and turn away whenever they hear frivolous talk, saying, 'We have our deeds and you have yours. Peace be with you! We do not seek the company of ignorant people'" (28:52–55). Here steadfastness, averting evil with good, charity, and avoidance of vain talk are attributed to the People of the Book; they also speak of themselves in terms of *islām*, describing themselves as "*muslimīn*" (translated "devoted ourselves to Him"). A double reward is promised to them. Elsewhere, the Qur'ān also talks about a group among the People of the Book who are a balanced community, as distinct from many who are evildoers (5:66).

The Qur'ān explicitly underlines the holiness of the places of worship and rites of the adherents of other religious traditions; it is not only in mosques that the name of God is commemorated, but in monasteries, synagogues, and churches as well (22:40). Furthermore, the Qur'ān clearly states that in the Torah there is guidance and light and that Christians must judge by their book. Then, after mentioning the Qur'ān, the same passage concludes: "We have assigned a law and a path to each of you. If God had so willed, He would have made you one community, but He wanted to test you through that which He has given you, so race to do good: you will return to God and He will make clear to you the matters you differed about" (5:44–48).

In a more direct and also inclusive manner the following verse talks about religious diversity: "The [Muslim] believers, the Jews, the Christians, and the Sabians—all those who believe in God and the Last Day and do good—will have their rewards with their Lord. No fear for them, nor will they grieve" (2:62). Commentators have made extensive attempts to clarify the meaning of this verse and particularly to whom it refers—who are "the believers" and "the

Sabians"? But apart from these technical exegetical issues, it is clear that the Qur'ān is according validity to other religions and emphasizing that the main criteria of belief in God and the Last Day and righteousness are more important than religious affiliations. However, despite its clarity, this verse has traditionally been thought to be abrogated by another verse, which says: "If anyone seeks a religion other than *islam*: complete devotion to God, it will not be accepted by him: he will be one of the losers in the Hereafter" (3:85). Obviously, everything hinges upon the way in which *islam* is understood in this verse. If what is meant by it is Islam then other religions were only valid before the emergence of this particular tradition and hence the scope of its inclusiveness is severely limited. But if *islam* in the verse is taken to refer to *islām*, the minimal and essential attitude and view briefly described earlier, then the validity of other religions after the advent of Islam can be upheld.

Fortunately (from the point of view of those supporting a more inclusive Islamic theology), many exegetes, both traditional and contemporary, have judged that the alleged abrogation is not valid since, first, abrogation does not apply to those of God's sayings that include a promise of reward and, second, abrogation pertains to legal ordinances that are sometimes subject to change due to changing conditions.[7] Interestingly enough, Tabataba'i does not discuss the issue of abrogation at all, preferring to emphasize again that "the criterion and reason for moral nobility and ultimate felicity is a genuine faith in God and the Last Day and good deeds. . . . None of these names [religious affiliations and labels] benefit their bearers and no quality leads to salvation except adherence to humble veneration of God (*'ubudiyya*)."[8] Moreover, the validity of other religious traditions acknowledged in 2:62 is explicitly confirmed by 5:69, which parallels 2:62 almost exactly; the differences between the two verses are minute. Therefore, one can argue that if 2:62 was abrogated by 3:85 it is reinstated by 5:69. Another way in which some commentators have sought to circumscribe the application of the verse is to ascribe the occasion of the revelation of the verse to a specific group. However, this can be refuted by the argument that the occasion of revelation generally sheds light on the conditions under which the verse was revealed and does not limit its application only to the specific incident, otherwise many Qur'ānic teachings would have to be regarded as no longer relevant. Ultimately, the verse cannot be regarded as abrogated because the *islām* mentioned in 3:85 can be shown to refer to *islām* rather than Islam, as I shall argue presently.

There are two verses in which the word *islām* appears that can be used in an argument to delimit the applicability of the inclusive or even pluralist verses mentioned above: these are 3:85, referred to earlier, and 3:19. The latter says: "True religion, in God's eyes, is *islām* . . . Those who were given the Scripture disagreed out of rivalry, only after they had been given knowledge—if anyone denies God's revelations, God is swift to take account." Taking into consideration the verses before and after this verse makes it vividly apparent that the *islām* mentioned in this verse clearly refers to the general belief in the one God and submission and devotion to him that are the central elements of *islām* rather than Islam. Of particular significance here is the following verse: "If they argue with you [Prophet], say, 'I have devoted myself to God alone and so have my followers.' Ask those who were given the Scripture, as well as those without one, 'Do you too devote yourselves to Him alone?' If they do, they will be guided, but if they turn away, your only duty is to convey the message. God is aware of His servants" (3:20).

The other verse, 3:85, is also worth considering again in this connection, this time together with the two preceding verses, which supply the context within which it can be understood:

> [83] Do they seek anything other than submission to God? Everyone in the heavens and earth submits to Him, willingly or unwillingly; they will all be returned to him. [84]Say [Muhammad], "We [Muslims] believe in God and in what has been sent to us and to Abraham, Ishmael, Isaac, Jacob, and the Tribes. We believe in what has been given to Moses, Jesus, and all the prophets by their Lord. We do not make a distinction between any of the [prophets]. It is to Him that we devote ourselves." [85]If anyone seeks a religion other than *islām*: complete devotion to God, it will not be accepted by him: he will be one of the losers in the Hereafter.

First, 3:83 refers to the submission of everything to God (ontological or *takwīnī* submission). Next, 3:84 refers to the devotion of all prophets to Him (religious or *tashrī'ī* submission). This leads to 3:85, which speaks of the general devotion or submission that is essential for salvation, according to the concluding part of this last verse. The context shows very clearly what is meant by *islām* in these verses.

In some interesting verses the Qur'ān denounces the religious exclusivism of certain groups among the Jews and Christians of the time of revelation. Thus a group of Jews is said to claim that they alone are "friends of God" (62:6).

Such exclusivism is rejected more directly as "wishful thinking" (*amānī*) in the following passage:

> They also say, "No one will enter Paradise unless he is a Jew or a Christian." This is their own wishful thinking. [Prophet], say, "Produce your evidence if you are telling the truth." In fact, any who direct themselves wholly [*man aslama wajhahu*] to God and do good will have their reward with their Lord: no fear for them, nor will they grieve. The Jews say, "The Christians have no ground whatsoever to stand on," and the Christians say "The Jews have no ground whatsoever to stand on," though they both read the Scripture, and those who have no knowledge say the same; God will judge between them on the Day of Resurrection concerning their differences. (2:111–13)

The interesting point here is the use of *aslama*, a word cognate with *islām*. The emphasis is again clearly on devotion to God and good deeds as the main constituents of a guaranteed and safe future. To forestall Muslims from thinking that they may be exempt from the admonition mentioned in response to the exclusivism of the Jews, the Qur'ān is quick to say:

> But we shall admit those who believe and do good deeds into Gardens graced with flowing streams, there to remain forever—a true promise from God. Who speaks more truly than God? It will not be according to your hopes or those of the People of the Book: anyone who does wrong will be requited for it and will find no one to protect and help him against God; anyone, male or female, who does good deeds and is a believer, will enter paradise and will not be wronged by as much as the dip in a date stone. Who could be better in religion than those who direct themselves wholly to God, do good, and follow the religion of Abraham, who was true in faith? God took Abraham as a friend. (4:122–25)

Again here the Qur'ān underlines *islām* as devotion and good deeds, characteristic of Abraham.[9]

Beyond the rejection of exclusivism in any religious tradition there seems to be a more profound pluralistic approach to religious diversity in the Qur'ān. In this category of verses one can find an approval of the plurality of religions and even strong indications that this plurality should be seen as part of God's plan or providence. One such verse is: "Each community has its own direction to which it turns: race to do good deeds and wherever you are, God will bring you together. God has power to do everything" (2:148). We have already noted the end of 5:48: "We have assigned a law and a path to each of you. If God had so willed, He would have made you one community."[10] In such verses a particular religious way of life (*mansak, manhaj* or *shir'a*) is assigned to each community, which is valid and efficacious as long as the main elements of salvation captured by the word *islām* are present in it. Also of special importance in this context is a verse in which the Qur'ān speaks of an irrevocable diversity among people: "If your Lord had pleased, He would have made all people a single community, but they continue to have their differences" (11:118).

Although we have already discussed the main characteristics of *islām*, it seems appropriate to elaborate on them further. Many verses can help clarify what *islām* means more concretely in terms of elements necessary for salvation, but one verse in particular is immensely important as it explains the meaning of righteousness, to which we have already frequently referred:

> Righteousness does not consist in turning your face towards East or West. The truly good are those who believe in God and the Last Day, in the angels, the Scripture, and the prophets; who give away some of their wealth, however much they cherish it, to their relatives, to orphans, the needy, travellers and beggars, and to liberate those in bondage; those who keep up the prayer and pay the prescribed alms; who keep pledges whenever they make them; who are steadfast in misfortune, adversity, and times of danger. These are the ones who are true, and it is they who are godfearing. (2:177)[11]

This verse clearly downplays the ultimate role of some contingent religious rites and highlights specific practical attitudes, revolving around unselfishness, compassion, patience, and the fear of God. As usual in the Qur'ān, belief and action, orthodoxy and orthopraxis, are interconnected.[12]

The majority of Muslim commentators, however, have not accepted the view advocated here and have tried in various ways, some of which have been discussed earlier, to avoid embracing a pluralistic position on religious diversity. One important way of doing so has been to regard other religions as valid and legitimate only before the coming of Islam. This seems to me a very strange approach requiring the unacceptable stretching of the obvious meaning of so many Qur'ānic verses that can simply and straightforwardly be interpreted in a pluralistic sense. One relevant question here is this: If the approbation and praise addressed to Christians and Jews in so many Qur'ānic verses was due to their conversion to Islam and acceptance of it as the final revelation, then why

does the Qur'ān still call them the People of the Book? The majority interpretation seems to fly in the face of the obvious meaning of the text.

To maintain the argument presented in this chapter, it is necessary for some
verses that may be thought to imply a different perspective to be interpreted in
the light of these pluralistic verses. For example, 3:110, addressing the Muslims,
says: "You are the best community singled out for people." However, the context clearly shows that such superiority is not related to teachings or attitudes
essentially absent in other traditions as the Qur'ān immediately connects this
superiority to the moral quality of ordering what is right and forbidding what
is wrong. This is among the essential qualities of *islām* discussed above and,
therefore, if any other religious community practices it that community can
also be superior. As we saw earlier, this quality was in fact ascribed to certain
groups among the People of the Book at 3:114. Conversely, if Muslims do not
practice it they will automatically be deprived of that superiority.

Another verse that can be invoked to endorse a nonpluralist view in the
Qur'ān is 6:19: "This Qur'ān was revealed for me to warn you and everyone it
reaches." This may be interpreted as implying a universal validity of Islam to
the exclusion of other religions. In response, however, one can refer to 42:7,
where the Qur'ān says: "So we have revealed an Arabic Qur'ān to you, in order
that you may warn the capital city and all who live nearby," thus counterbalanc-
ing the alleged universality of 6:19. Furthermore, at least one other valid possibility is to attribute the universality of the message of the prophet to its central
aspects, namely *islām*, rather than to the totality of Islam with all its specificities.
The same can be said of the Qur'ān's description of itself as "a message for all
people" and of the prophet as a "mercy to all people" (81:27; 21:107). In the
same manner, verses such as 5:57 in which Muslims are told not to take Jews
and Christians as allies can be interpreted as reflecting a contingent historical
situation with respect to a particular group of "wrongdoers," as the end of this
verse suggests. This instruction is thus not applicable to all Jews and Christians.

A comprehensive approach to the Qur'ān can substantiate the view that the
text makes a distinction between, on the one hand, some essential and minimal
teachings and a set of moral and spiritual attitudes and values closely linked to
them, which can be called *islām*, and, on the other hand, the historical manifestations or expressions of those essential components of salvation in the various
forms of human religiosity with all their particularities, such as Judaism, Christianity, and Islam. Universality is accorded to *islām* rather than to the various

historical expressions. My conclusion is therefore that, according to the Qur'ān, *islām* is universal whereas Islam is particular, and that there is no logical contradiction here.

Notes

1. Muhammad Husayn Tabataba'i, *al-Mīzān fī tafsīr al-Qur'ān*, 20 vols (Beirut, 1974), 5:358.
2. Ibid., 3:304.
3. Ibid., 3:440.
4. Ibid., 4:91.
5. Ibid., 19:173.
6. Ibid., 6:81–82.
7. Abu Ja'far Muhammad ibn al-Hasan al-Tusi, *al-Tibyān fī tafsīr al-Qur'ān*, 8 vols (Beirut, 1379/1960), 1:284–285; al-Sheikh Abu Ali al-Fazl ibn al-Hasan al-Tabarsi, *Majma' al-bayān fī tafsīr al-Qur'ān*, 10 vols (Beirut, n.d.), 1:244.
8. Tabataba'i, *Mīzān*, 1:193.
9. See also 2:135 and 3:67.
10. See also 16:93; 22:34; 22:67; 42:8–9.
11. The translation by Abdel Haleem, followed throughout this essay, has been altered here at two points: the first word "Righteousness" replaces "Goodness," and "godfearing" replaces the final phrase "aware of God."
12. See also sūra 107.

1.2 Particularity, Universality, and Finality
Insights from the Gospel of John

DANIEL A. MADIGAN

That impressive array of abstract nouns in our section title—three -ities and one -ation—certainly puts us at high risk of falling into a morass of philosophical abstraction! Yet these words touch on some of the central issues and most concrete claims of our respective faiths. They are the vocabulary of confident and uncompromising faith, and so they often raise the thorniest of questions when it comes to the relations between believers of different traditions. What I hope to do here is to explore how Christians can use this vocabulary in a way that is fully consonant with Christian faith, yet without the arrogance or dismissal that has often been heard in these terms. In short, I have in the back of my mind at each turn whether, and if so how, we can use this kind of language in a way that opens up dialogue rather than barring the way to it.

I intend to take as the framework of my remarks John's Gospel, for I think it is fair to say that, among the Gospel writers, it is John who has the most explicit and elaborate theology of revelation. As "hooks" upon which to hang this presentation, I will take four of John's key phrases: "In the beginning was the Word" (1:1); "The Word was made flesh and dwelt among us" (1:14); "It is accomplished" (19:30); and "Receive the Holy Spirit" (20:23).

In the Beginning

Although the three concepts of particularity, universality, and finality are somehow inseparable when it comes to talk of revelation, let us try to focus on each one at a time, beginning with the notion of universality. And where better to begin than where John does, echoing the book of Genesis, "in the beginning," at the universe's creation. In the beginning, the Word already existed with God.

The Word is intrinsic to God—that is to say, a god without anything to say would not be God at all. Because of its being intrinsic to God, the divine Word is, like God, eternal and not simply part of God's creation. This is the first facet of the Word's universality: it is eternal and thus precedes the particularity of creation.[1]

The Word is also unitary. As God's Word, it is not simply a series of words but a unified and coherent truth—God's truth about God's self. As such it is not just one word of truth among many; it is the originating truth of all that is, and thus it is unique. We might say it is the only Word with a capital W, because as John puts it, "What God was, the Word was" (1:1).[2] While the Word was not simply identifiable with God—because John twice stresses that the Word was in relationship to God (*pros ton theon*)—still was it nothing other than divine. Arabic speakers might notice a similarity to the phrase used about God's speech (*kalām*) by Muslim theologians: *lā 'aynuh wa-lā ghayruh*—"neither identical with [God], nor other than [God]."

Yet this truth does not remain simply hidden in God. It is expressed in creation. As John puts it, "Through [the Word] all things came to be; and nothing that has come into being came into being except through [the Word]" (1:3). He is referring to God's repeatedly saying, "let there be . . ." in the Genesis 1 account of creation, and the answering "and it was so." Since everything was created through the Word, all of creation has, as it were, that Word woven into the fiber of its being. Here we would want to make a distinction: it is not that creation is infused with the Word, because that would imply the creation had some existence without the Word, and the Word has been added to it as to an empty container. Rather, the Word is inwoven: the Word is part of the very stuff of creation's existence. For this reason creation itself reveals what God is communicating, since it is already a vehicle of God's self-expression. This is a further sense of the Word's universality.

The role of the Word in creation also implies that there is a universal intelligibility of the Word to the created order. Creation could be said to have been made in order to resonate with the Word of God. That is to say, creation is to be the means of expressing that Word, and also is to be addressed by it. God's commanding word "Be!" is the beginning of a relationship: it is only the first word, not the last. Thus God's Word is never a foreign language to God's creation. At a very fundamental level it is the universal language.

If nonhuman creation is seen as universally obedient to the commanding word of God—God said, "Let there be . . ." and so it was (Genesis 1:3, 6, 9, 11, 14, 20, 24)—the human beings made in the image and likeness of God are assuredly not so. The first part of Genesis, to which John has directed our attention with his opening words, portrays the unfolding of a human history alienated from God by its own choice. The divine Word that ordered and set limits for the good of creation is felt by human beings to be a confining word, an unreliable word, a word that would defraud man and woman of the divine status they are for some reason convinced is rightly theirs (Genesis 3:4). The word of the tempter seems much more trustworthy.

As John sees it in the Prologue to his Gospel—and in this he is apparently reflecting a consistent strain in the Jewish thought of his time[3]—God's Word is repeatedly addressed to the world in order to restore the intimate relationship with creation that had characterized the beginning of our history, but which was ruptured by humanity's refusal of God's authority. We might have expected that, since the world is constituted by God's Word, it would always have resonated with and thrilled to that Word. And we might have hoped that, when God addressed humanity, it would be as though the Word were coming home. Yet it is not so. The Word, John says, "was in the world—the very world that had its being through [the Word]—and yet the world did not recognize [the Word]. [The Word] came to its own, yet [the Word's] own people did not accept [the Word]" (John 1:10–11).

Yet alongside this almost universal rejection of the Word, there is a particular history of positive response. There are those, John tells us, who do recognize the Word and respond to it. Those people are enabled by that Word to enter once more into our original and real relationship with God—that is to say, we recognize our true origin in God and in God's creative will. Those who return to the right relationship with God recognize that their true origin does not lie in those other forces to which we are often inclined to attribute it in a reductionist manner: biology ("blood"), sexuality ("the will of the flesh"), or the human desire to perpetuate oneself ("the will of man") (John 1:13). The major figures of the history of positive response to the Word with whom John is familiar would be Noah, Abraham, Moses, and the other prophets. Yet he does not limit the Word's activity to the particular history of Israel. The Word did not just come once, but it is the continuing nature of the Word—perhaps that is the strength of John's use of the participle *erchomenos*—to be coming into the world.

Particularity

Mention of Noah, Abraham, and Moses brings us into the realm of particularity. Yet particularity had already begun with the act of creation. God's creation, as pictured in Genesis, involves at each step God's imagining, deciding, and acting. The Word, even at the most universal level of the creation, shows itself to be not simply an abstract universal but a very particular, concrete Word, a Word that has called into being a particular world. The universe God created through the Word could have been different from what it is.

In order to address concrete persons and situations in this particular world, that eternal, unitary and universal Word, with a capital W, must be expressed in a particular language. Until it is, it remains a speech entirely internal to God. This concrete particularity of language is essential to any communication, yet at the same time it conditions that communication because of its grounding in a culture and history.

This is always a delicate point for those of us who believe in revelation. Is the divine Word so compromised by the particularity necessary to God's communication with humanity that we can no longer claim it to be universal? Do we have to accept that the eternal Word of God remains as abstract and distant as an unexpressed idea? Few believers would accept that! Do we have to consider that the particular revelation to which we bear witness is just one among a number of partial and limited revelations, none of which on its own, and perhaps not even all of them together, can be the full expression of what God wishes to communicate to us? Few of us would be content to do so.

We often work from within a philosophy that distinguishes between an "abstract universal" as the essence of the thing—for example "chairness" or "shoeness"—and the limited instantiations of those universal essences in concrete particulars, like the range of actual chairs or actual shoes in this room.

Yet there is what seems to me a more pragmatic philosophy—even though it is often associated with the British Idealists and their reading of Hegel—a philosophy that might suit us better, and that speaks of "concrete universals."[4] A concrete universal is something that itself embodies the essence in a complete way, and thus becomes the measure or paradigm against which all other particulars, with their shortcomings or imperfections, are judged. So this concrete universal is both particular—because it is concrete—and universal, because it is perfect and paradigmatic. This is characteristic of the claims we make in our traditions about the Word of God as we perceive it. What we believe has been given to us as God's Word is necessarily incomparable and all other claims to have heard the Word will be measured against it. We shall return to this when we speak of finality.

For John's Gospel and for the Christian tradition generally, the particular language chosen for the Word's concretely universal address to the world is what he refers to as "flesh" (John 1:14), and this brings us to our second textual "hook." "The Word was made flesh and pitched his tent among us"; that is to say, God's Word was spoken to us in an *embodied* language, or even, we might say, in body language. It is essential to understanding the Christian notion of the incarnation—the term derives from this very verse of John—to think of "flesh" as a language rather than as simply the body of a speaker. And when we speak of "flesh" in this case, Christians do not mean only a body, but rather a human person, the person of Jesus of Nazareth. The Word is expressed not simply through the words of the person Jesus but through his being and action. His entire life—the living, the dying, and the rising—is the message; he is for Christians not simply the messenger.

In that same verse John goes on to say, "and we saw his glory, the glory as of a father's only child, full of grace and truth." This introduces two ideas that will become central to his Gospel and to Christian faith: "only-begotten" and "father." Yet these terms have raised issues between Muslims and Christians that have divided us for centuries. I can scarcely avoid talking about them here, but I do not have the time to dwell on them at great length. What may be helpful here is to focus the discussion on the relationship of God's Word to God's self, a complex question also for Muslims.

Christians use the image of begetting to express this relationship precisely because we want to insist that God and God's Word have the same nature. The Word is not God's creation in time; rather it is God's eternal self-expression— what by some Muslim theologians is called *kalām nafsī*, literally "self-speech" or "personal speech"—and at various times and in various ways this speech is spoken in the world as *kalām lafzī*, "speech in words."[5] Of course, in using the metaphor of begetting we now recognize that a parent and a child do not have the same nature, but only similar, related natures—and to this extent our image is inadequate.[6] Yet we feel we must maintain the analogy of begetting in order to avoid the worse inadequacies of implying either that the Word is created in time, and so has its own separate nature, or even worse that it has its own separate nature and is uncreated—for that would mean that the Word is a separate divinity. Such a thing neither of our communities would accept.

Any of the languages in which God might choose to communicate with humanity is necessarily a human language—otherwise it would not be communication. This is so not only because language requires organs of speech and hearing—or their analogical equivalents in the case of the deaf. Speech exists in a cultural matrix that gives a consensual meaning to the sounds and structures. In this sense, it might be considered no more scandalous that God should speak in body language than the Hebrew or Arabic language. If God is capable of communicating through one or other of those human mediums, God is no less capable of expressing himself through a human life.

We know that Muslims find it difficult to understand how Christians can think of Jesus as in any sense divine. Yet in many respects what Christians are doing is not so different from what Muslims are doing. We are both recognizing the presence and expression of the eternal, universal, divine Word in something that, to someone who does not believe, is merely human—in the case of Christians, in a first-century carpenter from Nazareth; in the case of Muslims, in a seventh-century Arabic text.[7] The only appropriate response when confronted with what seems to us to be God's Word is the obedience of faith. Neither Christian nor Muslim feels entitled to dispute or reduce the status of the Word-come-among-us. While we both recognize that God has necessarily chosen a human language in order to communicate with us, we do not for that reason reject the divine nature of the Word addressed to us.

God's speech to humanity is always in a certain sense vulnerable because it can be forgotten, ignored, or scoffed at, dismissed as "tales of the ancients," or as lies—to use some of the charges that the Qur'ān says are hurled against the Word when it comes to people. What for Christians, however, is particular and essential in the embodied nature of God's speech is that that vulnerability, too, is embodied. The rejection is felt, borne, suffered, and, most importantly, responded to with forbearance and forgiveness. As human beings, we have been given the freedom to accept or reject God's Word. In Jesus, God's Word—which is not something other than God—begs our acceptance and bears the brunt of our rejection.

I recall a student in the Qur'ān department at Ankara University asking me, when I had explained the idea of flesh as language, whether it didn't make more sense for God to use straightforward words of an ordinary language in order to speak to us clearly, rather than the ambiguous "language" of human living and action, which after all could be interpreted in so many ways. It struck me as a fair and sensible question, even if a little naïve about the complexity of interpreting written texts. As sometimes happens at such moments, the insight her question catalyzed in me took me by surprise. It depends on the message, I told her. If the message consists of direction and instruction, the more straightforward the language, the better. If, however, the message is of love, forgiveness, and reconciliation, then as human beings we recognize that our gestures, our actions, our vulnerability—that is to say, our body language—speaks much more clearly than the finest of words. What we do in the flesh is often more revealing of interior disposition than are the words that come from our lips.

The Word of God that Christians perceive to be revealed in Jesus is not a series of directives that need to be stated in clear and unambiguous terms. It is the revelation of God's gracious, forgiving love. Talk is cheap, we rightly say, especially if it is talk about love. To embody love, on the other hand, costs everything.

God's Word in Jesus Christ is not primarily a word of information nor a word of command, but a word that effects something. The same Word that created our humanity comes to us in that humanity. The Word does not simply communicate to us something *about* God but it performs being God, because the Word is not other than God—*lā ghayruh*. The Word acts out what it is to be divine in a way hitherto only glimpsed, but now made dramatically evident— and not just evident, but effective. The Word also plays out what it is to be truly human, what a humanity that fully resonated with God's Word would look like.

It is here that universality, particularity, and finality link together in the Christian understanding. The love of God is universal, yet to express that love completely, in a way that goes beyond mere generalities, God chose (had to choose?) a particular historical moment and situation to embody and live out that love, which like all love is vulnerable. Indeed it makes itself vulnerable, for love is unprotected, disarmed. It would even lay down life itself rather than respond to the beloved's rejection with hatred, returning evil for evil.

Finality

This brings us to the third Johannine "hook." It is on the Cross, just at the point of death that Jesus says, "It is accomplished" (*tetelestai*) (19: 30). But what is accomplished? What is brought to completion? What has become final? And how so? There are various senses in which completeness or finality can be understood.

First, it is the Word's mission to reveal God, and Christians are those who see that mission carried out as completely as it can be in this supreme act of vulnerable, self-sacrificing, disarmed love. If it has always been the mission of the Word to reconnect the world with the creator and reestablish the original harmony between God and God's creation, then here in the Cross that mission is accomplished. The Word has succeeded in entering most fully into our humanity, even to the point of sharing that peculiarly human fate of having one's goodness and love misunderstood and rejected, and of being unjustly put to death. It is seen by Christians as being final also in the sense of being *unsurpassable* because the love revealed here knows no limit.

It is also final in the sense of being *irrevocable*. What God has spoken is spoken once and for all, and things can never again be as though God had not spoken. There is no turning back the clock. The universal Word has finally been spoken in all its particularity and specificity in our concrete history, and so our human history will never be the same again.

There is a further sense in which our human history can never be the same again: a human being, one like us, has given himself over freely and completely to the divine Word that sought to express itself through him. This effects a union, or reunion, between God and humanity; that is, if you like, the kernel of the renewal of creation that God is effecting. Creation needs renewing, not because God failed, but because the process of humanity's creation was taken over and, as it were, shut down by human beings themselves. Because of our refusal of that harmonious relationship with God imaged in the Genesis accounts of creation, because we would not hear God's Word as bearing only blessing and the promise of fuller life, we used our freedom to withdraw from the divine project for humanity. We set about constructing that nightmare of alienation that our world has so often been—alienation from God, from one another, and from the rest of creation. In Jesus, God definitively turns toward the world, even though the world continue to turn away. In Jesus, humanity turns definitively toward God, however much we resist entering into that renewed relationship.

Finality Initiated

Yet there are other senses of "final" and "complete" that are not appropriate to our understanding of revelation. And here is our fourth "hook" from John: when Jesus appeared to his disciples after his resurrection he breathed on them and said, "Receive the Holy Spirit" (John 20:23). He had already said to them during the farewell discourse of the Last Supper. "I have many more things to say to you, but you are not able to bear them now. However, when the Spirit of truth comes, he will guide you into all truth" (John 16:12–13a). It is not possible to discuss here the interpretation that some Muslims give to this verse as a prophecy of the coming of the Prophet of Islam. In a *Christian* context, this saying is indication enough that although the definitive revelation may have already taken place in the Word-made-flesh, the full significance of it will only gradually become clear, and only to those who allow God's spirit to guide them to the full truth of that revelation. So finality is begun, but not yet finished.

Any claim to completeness and finality, from whichever tradition it might come, seems to most people not just monopolistic; that is, a claim to have cornered the market on something of which others stand in need. It also appears a rashly pretentious claim to have completely appropriated what God has revealed, whereas the process of understanding and receiving what God has revealed is very gradual. Terms like "complete," "final," or "full" can give much too static a sense of revelation, and also of salvation, as a transaction finished and done with rather than as a relationship that has been established and that continues. The correct attitude of a believer before what she or he considers to be God's definitive Word is not one of pride in the possession of this revelation, but rather humility before it. The truth of God will possess us, and not vice versa. We are servants of that Word and that Truth, not its masters or owners.

In much Christian talk about other religious traditions the same static approach seems to come through. The "rays of truth" (Vatican II, *Nostra aetate* §2) and "seeds of the Word" (*Ad Gentes* §11) that Christians maintain are to be found in those traditions do not seem to be thought of as still living and productive. Rather they are spoken of as though they had reached the limits of their usefulness—faded rays, shriveled seeds—and had stopped short of effecting a real recognition and flowering of the truth of God's Word.

It is true that Christians are not awaiting some further revelation of God not already made known to us in the Christ event. However, we can be helped by the activity of the Spirit beyond the Church, and by the presence of "seeds of the Word" in other traditions, to realize ever more fully what has already been expressed in Christ, but not yet fully appropriated. Recent Catholic teaching has wanted to insist that there is no separate activity of the Word unrelated to the Word-made-flesh.[8] From this it follows that there will be a resonance between, on the one hand, the activity of the Word in diverse religious traditions, and on the other, what has been revealed in Christ. In those resonances, the Spirit, who Jesus promised would lead his followers into all truth, may be calling Christians through the other religions to a deeper penetration into the mystery of Christ, who we believe reveals for us the mystery of God. In that sense, other religious traditions are not extra truths or alternative truths,[9] but they can assist Christians toward a fuller appreciation of the one truth. If, as the Second Vatican Council maintains (*Gaudium et spes* §16), other traditions are to be considered a *praeparatio evangelica*—a preparation for God's Good News—then surely they can also prepare Christians to hear the Gospel more thoroughly.

Before concluding, I want to make one more observation. There is an important distinction to be maintained between two senses of universality. As sometimes understood, universality refers to the goal of our respective activities of proclamation and preaching, of mission and *da'wa*. We hope that the beliefs and the way of life we propose will eventually become universal. In a quite different sense, universality refers to our belief that a particular, decisive event has a universal significance, even if that significance is still not universally recognized. Christians are sometimes thought of—and perhaps we often think of ourselves—as promoters of a way of life we hope will eventually become universal. We work to convince as many as possible to follow our list rather than someone else's list of the things you have to do or not do if you want God to love you and save you. However, it is a mistake to see the Gospel as a series of taboos to be avoided or rituals and duties to be performed in order to keep God content. The Gospel is not about what we *have to do* in order to be worthy of God's love. It is, rather, about what God *has done* for love of us even though we were not, and still are not, worthy of that love. It is about a particular act in a particular time and place that we have come to believe has universal significance.

But it was not *our* act, or *our* doing. God is not *our* God. Jesus the Word was not a Christian. We are not to be the proprietors or custodians of that event, controlling access to it, or profiting from our knowledge of it. We are not to monopolize that event but rather to allow ourselves to be transformed by it. We are to witness to it by living that same kind of self-sacrificing love. Wherever else we see such love in action we will welcome it and proclaim that it, too, is revealing of God and of the true meaning of God's creation. To put that in Qur'ānic terms: all self-sacrificing love is an *āya*, a sign that reveals God to us. Christians are proclaiming that what God has effected in Jesus Christ has universal significance, even though we ourselves may be poor witnesses to him.

Conclusion

It is tempting to think that we can proceed step by simple step from universality, through particularity to finality. However, I hope it has become clear that these three elements do not simply follow on from one to the next. They interact with and play off one another. It is axiomatic that—for a Christian—Jesus, and in particular his Cross, is uniquely revealing of who God is. It is just as axiomatic for a Muslim that the Qur'ān is uniquely revealing of how God wants to be known. To return to the philosophical discussion from earlier in this paper, Jesus—for the Christian—and the Qur'ān—for the Muslim—is the *concrete universal*, the paragon against which anything else that might be thought to be revealing about God must be measured. There is no ignoring this difference, especially because the Qur'ān seems to rule out the significance of the Cross, not only as a uniquely revealing moment in the life of God, but by most accounts even as a historical event. This is where our particularities clash, and thus where the claims to universality and finality are also questioned. We can try to avoid the clash of our particularities and take refuge in vague, universal generalities, yet it is the particularities that make us who we are, and who we are is where dialogue begins.

Notes

1. Creation is also the point at which finality begins because God has committed himself to a particular creation. Once the Word is expressed in particularity, it is irrevocable. Even if God were to destroy what had been created, it would still have once existed and in that historical sense is final. God is still the God of that creation and the fact that it once existed is also revealing—as the Qur'ān often reminds its readers with regard to the civilizations that have passed away (e.g., Qur'ān 7:38; 13:30; 41:25; 46:18).

2. This translation is from the Revised English Bible. Biblical translations are otherwise my own.

3. See Daniel Boyarin, "The Gospel of the Memra: Jewish Binitarianism and the Prologue to John," in *Harvard Theological Review* 94.3 (July 2001), 243–84.

4. Rahner speaks of the "concrete absolute" as opposed to the "abstract absolute" when underlining the important distinction between a "religious monotheism" grounded in experience, and an abstract metaphysical monotheism. See his "The Oneness and Threefoldness of God in Discussion with Islam," in *Theological Investigations, Volume XVIII: God and Revelation* (New York, NY: Crossroads, 1978): 105–21.

5. Josef van Ess, *Theologie und Gesellschaft im 2. und 3. Jahrhundert Hidschra* (Berlin; New York: de Gruyter, 1997) Band IV, 615, 619.

6. The term *homoiousios* ("of a similar nature") was explicitly rejected as an alternative to the Nicene Creed's *homoousios* ("of the same nature") early in the Church's history.

7. This is not just some sleight-of-hand on the part of non-Muslims, an attempt to rethink Islam in Christian categories. Forty years ago the Iranian scholar Seyyed Hossein Nasr had recognized that it was a category mistake to compare the Gospel and the Qur'ān: "The word of God in Islam is the Quran; in Christianity it is Christ." Seyyed Hossein Nasr, *Ideals and Realities of Islam* (London: George Allen and Unwin, 1966; Second edition Unwin Paperbacks, 1979), 43.

8. Congregation for the Doctrine of the Faith, "Declaration *Dominus Iesus*: On the Unicity and Salvific Universality of Jesus Christ and the Church," §§4, 9, 11, 12.

9. *Dominus Iesus* strongly rejects such a notion (§§14, 21).

1.3   Revelation in Israel
Deuteronomy 7:1-11; Isaiah 49:1-6

ELLEN F. DAVIS

Deuteronomy 7:1–11

¹When the Lord your God brings you into the land that you are about to enter and occupy, and he clears away many nations before you—the Hittites, the Girgashites, the Amorites, the Canaanites, the Perizzites, the Hivites, and the Jebusites, seven nations mightier and more numerous than you—²and when the Lord your God gives them over to you and you defeat them, then you must utterly destroy them. Make no covenant with them and show them no mercy. ³Do not intermarry with them, giving your daughters to their sons or taking their daughters for your sons, ⁴for that would turn away your children from following me, to serve other gods. Then the anger of the Lord would be kindled against you, and he would destroy you quickly. ⁵But this is how you must deal with them: break down their altars, smash their pillars, hew down their sacred poles, and burn their idols with fire. ⁶For you are a people holy to the Lord your God; the Lord your God has chosen you out of all the peoples on earth to be his people, his treasured possession.

⁷It was not because you were more numerous than any other people that the Lord set his heart on you and chose you—for you were the fewest of all peoples. ⁸It was because the Lord loved you and kept the oath that he swore to your ancestors, that the Lord has brought you out with a mighty hand, and redeemed you from the house of slavery, from the hand of Pharaoh king of Egypt. ⁹Know therefore that the Lord your God is God, the faithful God who maintains covenant loyalty with those who love him and keep his commandments, to a thousand generations, ¹⁰and who repays in their own person those who reject him. He does not delay but repays in their own person those who reject him. ¹¹Therefore, observe diligently the commandment—the statutes and the ordinances—that I am commanding you today.

Isaiah 49: 1–6

> ¹Listen to me, O coastlands,
> pay attention, you peoples from far away!
> The Lord called me before I was born,
> while I was in my mother's womb he named me.
> ²He made my mouth like a sharp sword,

in the shadow of his hand he hid me;
he made me a polished arrow,
in his quiver he hid me away.
³And he said to me, "You are my servant,
Israel, in whom I will be glorified."
⁴But I said, "I have labored in vain,
I have spent my strength for nothing and vanity;
yet surely my cause is with the LORD,
and my reward with my God."

⁵And now the LORD says,
who formed me in the womb to be his servant,
to bring Jacob back to him,
and that Israel might be gathered to him,
for I am honored in the sight of the LORD,
and my God has become my strength—
⁶he says,
"It is too light a thing that you should be my servant
to raise up the tribes of Jacob
and to restore the survivors of Israel;
I will give you as a light to the nations,
that my salvation may reach to the end of the earth."

These two texts would seem to contradict one another. In Deuteronomy 7, Moses declares God's special (even unique) love for Israel and then goes on to mandate the destruction of the seven Canaanite nations that Israel will encounter in the land. By contrast, the prophet known as exilic (or "Second") Isaiah is charged with a ministry of restoration or reconciliation that extends beyond Israel: "I make you a light of nations" (*ûnĕtattîkā lĕ'ôr gôyîm*; Isaiah 49:6).[1]

Many if not most contemporary Christians would favor the second text as more adequately anticipating God's salvific action in Christ on behalf of all peoples. Indeed, many would say that the Deuteronomic proscription of the Canaanites has no part in the gospel message of the Christian Bible, as it is expressed in both Testaments. Yet when these two texts are read together (something I had not thought to do before they were assigned for this seminar) from a critical, historically informed perspective, it is evident that they have something in common: each articulates a theology of resistance to a dominant culture, a culture hostile to Israel's faith. The burden of divine revelation, conveyed through Moses and Isaiah respectively, is that God is with the people Israel precisely in their confrontation with the culture or nations that threaten them. I suggest that each passage has a distinctive and essential message to impart to Israel and to all worshipers of Israel's God as they may find themselves in similar social situations.

There is good historical reason to take offense at Deuteronomy 7—or rather, at how it has been used. The proscription of the Canaanites has been adduced to support the destruction of (among others) Native American tribes by European Americans, and Palestinian communities by Israeli Jews. Yet such usage seems to be entirely at odds with the social situation in which the passage was originally formulated and therefore with the contextual meaning of its forceful rhetoric. Deuteronomy likely was composed in the seventh century BCE, following the destruction of the northern kingdom of Israel by the Assyrians in 722. The Assyrians were the first great empire builders of the ancient Near East; they achieved cohesiveness by means of a policy of systematic identity erasure within conquered territories. In each case a very substantial portion of the native population was deported and replaced by groups brought in from elsewhere, with the result that all these displaced peoples gradually and permanently lost track of their histories, their traditions, their languages, and their religious identities. The so-called ten lost tribes of Israel were not an accident of history; they were a casualty of the imperial policy of identity erasure.

Moses assures Israel that if they keep the covenant, then God will "remove[2] . . . nations more numerous and powerful than you" (v. 1). Read against the background of the Assyrian policy, the assurances of divine removal and the covenantal stipulations that follow bespeak a stance and a strategy of resistance, aimed at preserving Israel's distinctive identity: "You shall not intermarry with them" (v. 3); "You shall tear down their altars and shatter their cultic pillars" (v. 5). Most offensive (in both senses of that word) is the charge to exterminate the Canaanites: "You shall impose on them a total ban; you shall neither make a covenant with them nor spare them" (v. 2). The charge is transparently directed at the Assyrian overlords and probably the populations they imported into Israelite territory. The notion of exterminating Canaanite nations was by the seventh century grossly anachronistic; the seven nations named here had disappeared from history centuries before—if indeed they had ever existed, which is doubtful with respect to several of them. Further, there is no archaeological evidence that Israelites ever exterminated Canaanite nations. More likely, the Israelites separated themselves both physically and ideologically from the Canaanite city-states in the plain of Sharon, settling for the most part peaceably in unwalled farming villages in the hill country, marginally arable land that the Canaanites were not eager to occupy.

Perhaps the single most important interpretive question to be asked about any literary text, including scripture, is the question of genre: "What do I read this *as*?" I suggest that both these texts are forms of resistance literature, a genre created by the weak who are in danger of being overwhelmed and annihilated, physically or culturally, by a stronger power. The resistance literature of the Bible was written by those without political and military power under conditions of domestic or foreign threat, and so it is appropriately used by and on behalf of those whose situations are similar. Read contextually, Deuteronomy 7, with its stated intention of exterminating the Canaanites, is the wishful thinking of the weak, the unarmed. We might disapprove of such a text—although for a militarily strong nation such as mine, that is probably the easy way out. Rather than condemning ancient Israelites, it is better to consider the real danger that attends appropriation of such a violently wishful text by the comparatively powerful, who may use it to endorse "realistic" programs of political and military oppression—programs that are often tragically successful.

Resistance can be sustained only within a relatively cohesive, if threatened, community, and so resistance literature characteristically evokes a shared memory, such as Moses at Sinai.[3] Moreover, if it is to fund a dream or plan that is not merely destructive, then the literature must provide solid grounds for hope and enduring faithfulness in the face of present suffering. Grounding resistance in those several ways constitutes much of the work of the Israelite prophets. Those whose voices are heard here, Moses and exilic Isaiah, are notably among the prophets most important for understanding the ministry of Jesus and consequently of the church.

As I have suggested, the essential grounding that comes from Deuteronomy concerns Israel's unique identity before God, namely as "a treasure-people" (*'am sĕgullâ*, v. 6)[4], whose chosen status proceeds solely from the love and faithfulness of God (v. 8). In turn, Israel is meant to love God, as mandated by the *Shema'*, "the first and great commandment" of Deuteronomy 6 (v. 4). A surprising discovery of modern biblical study is that the central term "love" was part of the political vocabulary of the ancient Near East. Probably it is no coincidence that in Assyrian treaties from the seventh century, "love" designates the exclusive devotion that vassal states owe to the Assyrian king or his son.[5] Taken together, then, Deuteronomy 6 and 7 make the clearest and most concise biblical statement about Israel's character: it is formed within a relationship of mutual love, which the biblical writers call "covenant." The relationship is religiously exclusive; Israel cannot participate in "Canaanite" (i.e., Assyrian-sponsored) family life, community, and worship—because those commitments would compete with the one covenant that gives Israel its identity.

So with respect to the vertical aspect of Israel's existence, the prophetic vision of Deuteronomy says something essential. On the horizontal axis, however, it is inadequate; Deuteronomy does not provide Israel with a way of relating positively and faithfully to the dominant cultures it faces. That is, it envisions no alternative to destruction on the one hand and apostasy on the other. Deuteronomy bespeaks what might be called a "ghetto mentality," which religious and political philosopher Rabbi David Hartman identifies as the refusal to admit the possibility that the larger culture could ever embrace or embody "any serious spiritual and ethical values."[6]

That possibility, however, seems to be implicit in Isaiah 49, in the proclamation that the servant Israel is to be "a light of nations." This prophetic poem comes from a later period of national weakness for Israel, after the southern kingdom of Judah (the remnant of greater Israel) had been destroyed by Nebuchadnezzar (586 BCE), and a substantial part of the population—likely including this prophet-poet—was living in exile in Babylon.

David Hartman contrasts the ghetto mentality with an attitude of "particularization"—that is, being open toward the world as a member of a minority, yet without being overwhelmed by the world. For Jews, Muslims, or Christians to embrace particularization as a religious goal would mean living among the nations (including each other), each of us with the confidence and dignity of our own religious identity, and with generosity toward others. Perhaps exilic Isaiah is the first prophet to give utterance to that kind of confidence:

> Listen, coastlands, to me,
> and attend, O nations far away:
> From the belly YHWH called me. . . .

The prophet's speech begins ostensibly as a public proclamation to the coastlands and nations—presumably, all those places where Judeans (Jews) have gone into exile. But it quickly becomes something more like a stage whisper;

the prophet seems to be speaking to himself and to the relatively few perhaps who overhear and take heed.

The vocation that the prophet claims is missional, though not in the sense that has become the standard among Western Christian missionaries, at least: people sent forth from a culture of power, sometimes well funded, aiming to convert. Rather, Isaiah testifies to a mission that emerges from weakness, from Israel's total collapse as a nation. Israel's mission is to be a source of blessing for all peoples; God's charge to Abraham—"Be a blessing!" (Genesis 12:2)—is here reiterated in exile. Contrary to all expectation, fulfillment begins to look like a real possibility only when God's "servant . . . Israel" (v. 3, cf. vv. 5, 6) has been tossed on the garbage heap of nations. Speaking for himself and presumably the people as a whole, the prophet despairs of the efforts he expended, presumably under better conditions:

> And *I* said, For emptiness I have labored;
> for waste and mist I have spent my strength.
> But now, my case rests with YHWH,
> and my work (*or* recompense) with my God. (v. 4)

The prophet witnesses to the reality that mission is not human work; it is God's work, and no small part of it is done precisely in and through human weakness and suffering. The four "Servant Songs" of Isaiah (42:1–9; 49:1–6; 50:4–9; 52:13–53:12) point to the powerful witness to God offered by those experienced in suffering and martyrdom—in the first instance, by exiled Judeans. But, as scholars have long noted, the identity of the servant remains elusive through these several poems: is it the prophet or another individual in Israel, or is it the whole people Israel? Christians have heard the voice and seen the figure of Jesus Christ in these songs, and by extension they have seen parts of the suffering church. The ambiguity is meaningful and essential to our understanding. No single answer suffices, because no faith, no ethnic group or nation has an exclusive or permanent claim to that privilege and responsibility of witnessing to Abraham's God through weakness and suffering. Isaiah ultimately speaks to and for all those who offer such a witness.

Notes

1. The Hebrew phrase *'ôr gôyîm* ("light of nations") is somewhat less explicit than its standard English rendering, "a light *to* the nations." While the passages from Deuteronomy

and Isaiah printed at the beginning of this chapter are from the New Revised Standard Version, the scriptural translations occurring within my comments are my own.

2. The verb *nāšal* is elsewhere used for removing a sandal from a foot; see Exodus 3:5 and Joshua 5:15.

3. On the communal character of sustained resistance, see Emmanuel M. Katongole, "Postmodern Illusions and the Challenges of African Theology: The Ecclesial Tactics of Resistance," *Modern Theology* 16:2 (April 2000): 248.

4. The noun *sĕgullâ* denotes primarily Israel as God's special possession; in late biblical literature, it denotes a king's material treasure (1 Chronicles 29:3 and Ecclesiastes 2:8).

5. See William L. Moran, "The Ancient Near Eastern Background of the Love of God in Deuteronomy," *Catholic Biblical Quarterly* 25 (1963), 80. See also Jon D. Levenson, *Sinai and Zion: An Entry into the Jewish Bible* (San Francisco: Harper & Row, 1985), 28, cf. 70–86.

6. David Hartman, "Particularization Not Ghettoization" (a publication of the Shalom Hartman Institute, Jerusalem, n.d.), 2.

1.4   Revelation in Israel
Qur'ān 2:47-57; 5:44-48

Qur'ān 2:47–57

[47]Children of Israel, remember how I blessed you and favoured you over other people. [48]Guard yourselves from a Day when no soul will stand in place of another, no intercession will be accepted from it, nor any ransom; nor will they be helped. [49]Remember when We saved you from Pharaoh's people, who subjected you to terrible torment, slaughtering your sons and sparing only your women—this was a great trial from your Lord—[50]and when We parted the sea for you, so saving you and drowning Pharaoh's people right before your eyes. [51]We appointed forty nights for Moses [on Mount Sinai] and then, while he was away, you took to worshipping the calf—a terrible wrong. [52]Even then We forgave you, so that you might be thankful.

[53]Remember when We gave Moses the Scripture, and the means to distinguish [right and wrong], so that you might be guided. [54]Moses said to his people, "My people, you have wronged yourselves by worshipping the calf, so repent to your Maker and kill [the guilty among] you. That is the best you can do in the eyes of your Maker." He accepted your repentance: He is the Ever Relenting and the Most Merciful. [55]Remember when you said, "Moses, we will not believe you until we see God face to face." At that, thunderbolts struck you as you looked on. [56]Then We revived you after you had died, so that you might be thankful. [57]We made the clouds cover you with shade and sent manna and quails down to you, saying, "Eat the good things We have provided for you." It was not Us they wronged; they wronged themselves.

Qur'ān 5:44–48

[44]We revealed the Torah with guidance and light, and the prophets, who had submitted to God, [and] the rabbis and the scholars all judged according to it for the Jews in accordance with that part of God's Scripture which they were entrusted to preserve, and to which they were witnesses. So [Children of Israel] do not fear people, fear Me; do not barter away My messages for a small price; those who do not judge according to what God has sent down are rejecting [God's teachings]. [45]In the Torah We prescribed for them a life for a life, an eye for an eye, a nose for a nose, an ear for an ear, a tooth for a tooth, an equal wound for a wound: if anyone forgoes this out of charity, it will serve as

atonement for his bad deeds. Those who do not judge according to what God has revealed are doing grave wrong.

[46]We sent Jesus, son of Mary, in their footsteps, to confirm the Torah that had been sent before him: We gave him the Gospel with guidance, light, and confirmation of the Torah already revealed—a guide and lesson for those who take heed of God. [47]So let the followers of the Gospel judge according to what God has sent down in it. Those who do not judge according to what God has revealed are lawbreakers.

[48]We sent to you [Muhammad] the Scripture with the truth, confirming the Scriptures that came before it, and with final authority over them: so judge between them according to what God has sent down. Do not follow their whims, which deviate from the truth that has come to you. We have assigned a law and a path to each of you. If God had so willed, He would have made you one community, but He wanted to test you through that which He has given you, so race to do good: you will all return to God and He will make clear to you the matters you differed about.

To grasp the full significance of the first of the above passages (2:47–57) for our understanding of the Qur'ānic idea of revelation, we need to relate it to other passages in the Qur'ān concerned with the same spiritual phenomenon but as seen from different perspectives. The Qur'ān speaks in many verses of revelations that came before it. Each different revelation is identified with a particular prophet and in some cases is also identified with a named book that is presented as its scriptural manifestation as, for example, in the case of Moses and the revelation of the Torah, and in the case of Jesus and the Gospel.

Belief in many divine revelations and therefore in many prophets and sacred books is central to the Islamic creed. Belief in all the revealed books and belief in all the messengers who are their respective recipients are two of the six fundamental articles of faith (*arkān al-īmān*). The Qur'ān mentions many specific revelations. But more important than this, the Qur'ān insists on the idea of the necessity and universality of revelation. The idea of the necessity of revelation is expressed in the Qur'ān in several ways. It is significant that in sūra 2, before the passage on the children of Israel under discussion here, we twice encounter the idea of the necessity of revelation, each time expressed in a different way. The first of these passages refers to "those who believe in the revelation sent down to you [Muhammad], and in what was sent before you" (2.4). This verse contains the doctrine of the multiplicity and spiritual continuity of revelations. It conveys the idea of the necessity of revelation since the doctrine of the multiplicity of revelations is a necessary consequence of *al-tawhīd*, the idea of the oneness of God.

It seems paradoxical for the Qur'ān to assert that since God is one, there must be many revelations, many prophets, and many sacred books. But multiplicity is a characteristic not just of the natural order but also of the human order. The Qur'ān speaks of the creation of a multiplicity of races, nations, and tribes (49:13), a human reality that necessitates the multiplicity and diversity of revelations. Furthermore, belief in the multiplicity of revelations is a defining characteristic of the God-conscious (*al-muttaqīn*) and is thus an integral element of God-consciousness (*taqwā*, 2:2–4). The idea of the necessity of revelation is implicit in this necessary connection between God-consciousness and faith in the multiplicity and spiritual continuity of revelations.

The second occurrence of the theme of the necessity of revelation is at 2:38: "We said, 'Get out, all of you! But when guidance comes from Me, as it certainly will, there will be no fear for those who follow My guidance nor will they grieve.'" This verse teaches the doctrine of the necessity of divine guidance for humanity, following the "fall" of Adam. Just as he, as the first human being, received revelation—and hence was also the first prophet—so also his descendants need revelation. The spiritual history of Adam narrated in verses 2:30–38 culminates in the divine assurance that God's guidance will definitely come to Adam's descendants.

But if revelation is necessary for human beings because of what they are as human beings, then it has to be universal. Thus the Qur'ān emphasizes the universality of revelation: "Every community is sent a messenger" (10:47). This verse emphasizes at once the multiplicity, universality, and unity of revelations. But we have also referred earlier to the particularity of revelations, which arises from the fact that the human community has grown diverse over the ages. The idea of the particularity of revelations is also alluded to in 5:44–48, the second passage under consideration here, particularly in verse 5:48: "We have assigned a law and a path to each of you." We may therefore say that each revelation is both particular and universal. The Qur'ān insists that the core message of every revelation is the same, namely worship of the One God.

The significance of the reference to the children of Israel in 2:47–57 (and more widely in sūra 2) is to be understood in light of, among other things, the Qur'ānic idea of revelation discussed above and the historical continuity of the "Abrahamic" revelations alluded to in 5:44–48. Reference to Israel in the selected passage provides a historical illustration of a universal truth, namely the spiritual continuity of divine revelations. It also illustrates God's blessings on different groups of humanity at different times in history. In His infinite mercy God has blessed all branches of the human family, but the blessings may take different forms in accordance with different times and places. The blessings of the children of Israel mentioned in the passage are not meant to support the idea of Israel as a chosen people. According to many commentators, the admonishment not to "sell My messages for a small price" (2:41) refers to the persistent Jewish belief that they alone among all nations had been graced by divine revelation. The Qur'ān consistently refutes the idea of "God's chosen people" on the basis of ethnicity.

There is a universal spiritual lesson to be learned from the religious history of the children of Israel with its many blessings and tribulations, just as there is a similar lesson to be learned from the religious histories of other peoples. But there are points of comparison that could be made between the religious histories of two peoples. In Qur'ānic perspective, what really matters is not the blessings that a community has received but how that community appreciates and responds to those blessings.

When looking at the long line of revelations and prophecies in the history of humanity, the Qur'ān appears to be interested in its position as the final revelation, both within the context of universal spiritual history and also within the more specific context of the spiritual history of the Abrahamic family of religions. The Prophet Muhammad closes the cycle of prophecy originating with Adam (33:40). The Qur'ān's claim to finality in the long series of revelations needs to be examined not on the basis of one or two verses but rather on the basis of its overall content, which, in the opinion of some Muslim scholars, represents the synthesis of all previous revelations.

1.5 Revelation in Christ
1 John 1:1–4; Matthew 28:16–20; John 16:12–15

1 John 1:1–4

¹We declare to you what was from the beginning, what we have heard, what we have seen with our eyes, what we have looked at and touched with our hands, concerning the word of life—²this life was revealed, and we have seen it and testify to it, and declare to you the eternal life that was with the Father and was revealed to us—³we declare to you what we have seen and heard so that you also may have fellowship with us; and truly our fellowship is with the Father and with his Son Jesus Christ. ⁴We are writing these things so that our joy may be complete.

Matthew 28:16–20

¹⁶Now the eleven disciples went to Galilee, to the mountain to which Jesus had directed them. ¹⁷When they saw him, they worshipped him; but some doubted. ¹⁸And Jesus came and said to them, "All authority in heaven and on earth has been given to me. ¹⁹Go therefore and make disciples of all nations, baptizing them in the name of the Father and of the Son and of the Holy Spirit, ²⁰and teaching them to obey everything that I have commanded you. And remember, I am with you always, to the end of the age."

John 16:12–15

¹²"I still have many things to say to you, but you cannot bear them now. ¹³When the Spirit of truth comes, he will guide you into all the truth; for he will not speak on his own, but will speak whatever he hears, and he will declare to you the things that are to come. ¹⁴He will glorify me, because he will take what is mine and declare it to you. ¹⁵All that the Father has is mine. For this reason I said that he will take what is mine and declare it to you."

The three New Testament passages considered here are all of great Christological and Trinitarian significance. They thus obviously raise issues that have been major points of division between Christians and Muslims. These passages also touch on two themes that are widely discussed in contemporary social reflection: innovation and globalization. However, whereas these themes would today be commonly understood in very secular terms, in these scriptural texts we are of course dealing with religious discussions of matters that were to prove determinative of the future development of the Christian community.

1 John 1:1–4

This opening passage of the first letter of John, in which there are many echoes of the prologue of John's Gospel, seems almost to be anticipating British empiricism in its emphasis on direct experience: "We declare to you what was from the beginning, what we have heard, what we have seen with our eyes, what we have looked at and touched with our hands." Here, however, the concern is with "the word of life" (v. 1). One of the issues addressed both in this passage and also toward the end of John's Gospel is the connection between the community of those who knew and actually touched the Lord and the community of believers more widely.

The Easter stories in the Gospels are nearly always fragmentary; they tell of brief encounters, suggesting the movement of the Lord into and out of the community of disciples. One of these stories, particularly cherished by many Christians, narrates the appearance of the risen Jesus a week after Easter to the disciples gathered together in the upper room and describes Thomas putting his hand into the side of the Lord, to confirm that this is indeed the same Jesus who was crucified. An important point made in that passage is that it is not only those who have seen who are blessed, because "blessed are those who have not seen and yet have come to believe" (John 20:24–29). So there is a fundamental parity between the situation of the believers who were the first witnesses and those who came later.

The same message of reassurance is present in this passage from the first letter of John, which speaks of how the revelation experienced by the original witnesses at a particular time in history is opened up to a widening circle of believers: "We declare to you what we have seen and heard so that you also may have fellowship with us; and truly our fellowship is with the Father and with his Son Jesus Christ" (v. 3). We find here an important aspect of the church's sense of itself, the experience of *koinonia* (here translated "fellowship"). The root concept of *koinonia* is of things being held in common. It is not a designation of kinship and significantly does not refer to family ties. *Koinonia* is with the Father and the Son, which is a fundamental source of Christian joy (v. 4).

So this passage includes a strong emphasis on the reality of the Incarnation—the Word made flesh—and its physical, tangible character. However, the significance of this foundational event is not limited to those who experienced it firsthand; rather, its significance continues to be renewed and made more widely available through the testimony of the witnesses. In terms of our concern with the theme of revelation, we thus see here a strong emphasis on particularity—the "word of life" revealed in a particular human person—and also movement in the direction of universality, as that which is particular is shared more widely through the growth of *koinonia.*

Matthew 28:16–20

In these concluding verses of Matthew's Gospel the disciples have come away from Jerusalem to encounter the risen Jesus in Galilee. This contrasts with the account in Luke's Gospel, where the concluding narratives are set in Jerusalem and its immediate environs. This contrast illustrates the important points both that the early Christian witness to the life and ministry of Jesus in the canonical Gospels is four-fold, and also that this witness is not in all respects perfectly harmonized, despite the earnest efforts of many Christians through the centuries to work everything into one harmonious story.

Verse 17 contains the interesting juxtaposition of two different responses among the disciples to the risen Jesus: doubt and worship. For the disciples to worship Jesus is for them to move beyond the relationship that they had to him as disciples during his active ministry, and in a direction that for Jews, and also for Muslims, would be theologically erroneous and even horrifying. The appropriateness of such worship is, however, implied by the words spoken by Jesus in v. 18 when he says: "All authority in heaven and on earth has been given to me."

There follow in v. 19 the words of Jesus that Christians have come to know as "the Great Commission," sending forth the eleven disciples to "make disciples of all nations." These words illustrate both the divine authority of Jesus and also the universal extent of the mission he entrusts to his community. This verse also speaks of baptism, using the Trinitarian formula, as the visible, sacramental sign of incorporation in the Christian community. The final verse then extends the mission of the disciples to teaching future disciples to obey everything that Jesus had taught them, adding the reassuring message that Jesus will be with them "always, to the end of the age."

Especially in the final two verses of this passage we can again discern the relationship between the particularity of what has been revealed in Jesus and the universal relevance of that revelation. That which had been made known in the ministry of Jesus and in the geographically and religiously limited context of Israel is now to be opened up to "all nations." Equally, the universal impulse in the mission that Jesus gives to his disciples is always to be informed by continuity with the particularity of what the disciples had learned from Jesus himself. Finally, we should note that significant considerations of time are suggested in the concluding words of this passage. If the presence of Jesus will extend "to the end of the age," this implies that what has been given in him is unsurpassable and that it bears upon the final condition of humanity.

John 16:12–15

These verses come from Jesus's "farewell discourses" to his disciples (John 13–17). These discourses are certainly a post-Easter construction, relatively late in the development of the New Testament. They represent a remarkable literary achievement, both highly abstract and yet deeply personal, containing a sense both of intimacy and of tension. They have been much cherished by Christians through the centuries.

Throughout these discourses there is a weaving of language that reiterates the Trinitarian character of the God who communicates to us in and through Jesus. Thus the same knowledge, the same properties, the same moral concerns are common to Father, Son, and Holy Spirit. And the *koinonia* that exists among them is the prototype for the *koinonia* that is to exist in the relationship between Jesus and the community of disciples.

There is particular significance for the present discussion in the words of Jesus in v. 12: "I still have many things to say to you, but you cannot bear them now." The sense here that the Gospel is somehow incomplete is echoed in its final verse (21:25) where it is said that if everything Jesus did were to be written down "the world itself could not contain the books that would be written."

From the same theological perspective, then, there is affirmation both of the finality of Jesus and also of the incompleteness of the Gospel. However, there will be substantial continuity as the disciples move forward into the future, for they will be guided by the Spirit "into all the truth" (v. 13). There will be continuity because the guidance of the Spirit is a matter neither of invention nor of departure from the original revelation or gift. Rather, the Spirit imparts what is common to the Father and the Son.

Turning now to more general observations arising from these texts, we note in them a strong eschatological element, pointing us to the end of time, the end of the age. In the New Testament as a whole, however, we find what twentieth-century theologians have described as a tension between the "already" and the "not yet." Jesus is recognized as the Christ, the Messiah, the anointed one, and yet the disciples found themselves, not simply on Easter morning but for the rest of their lives, living in a world that was not a Messianic world as they had envisioned it, not the renewed, reconciled world that Hebrew prophecy had led them to expect. But at the same time they are also conscious that eternal life has begun. As we have seen, the apostolic witness is to "the eternal life that was with the Father and was revealed to us" (1 John 1:2). So the Messianic age has indeed already begun in the passion, death, and resurrection of Jesus, and yet it is not fully accomplished. We therefore live in a time in-between, and for this we need a kind of interim guidance. This will influence both the ethic presented by the church and our understanding of the church itself.

And in the time between the first coming of Jesus and his definitive, final coming there stands a community, a bonding in a cosmopolitan world, bringing people together and transcending tribal boundaries. By the time of the composition of these texts—particularly the Johannine texts—this community has clearly broken away from the Jewish community and is in effect going forward into a largely unknown, unanticipated, surprising future, but with a considerable sense of confidence, which comes fundamentally from the gift of the Spirit.

The bonding at the heart of this community involves a redefinition of personal identity, so that people are in the first instance Christians, rather than Jews, Greeks, Romans, Scythians, or whoever else might be in the neighborhood. First-century cities such as Rome were highly cosmopolitan, and in this cosmopolitan world Christians could well be lost except for their strong sense of *koinonia* and the mutual love and support that were the chief virtues pursued within the Christian community. Of course with such *koinonia* there also comes a risk. Precisely because *koinonia* is immensely attractive and, in some respects, inclusive, it also runs the risk of becoming exclusive, because it is highly demanding and it can be taken over and misdirected by an exaggerated sense of opposition between "us" and "them," with the result that the negative and aggressive tendencies that are explicitly forbidden within the community get directed outward.

Finally, we move our focus from the place of the church in relation to the passage of time to the expansion of the church throughout the world. Especially in the passage from Matthew's Gospel, we see how the universal significance of the revelation of God in Christ gives rise to the profound missionary impulse within Christianity. This, of course, is a point of similarity between Christianity and Islam, and also in many parts of the world a source of considerable tension. In both traditions the missionary impulse has been very persistent and resilient. Christian missionary activity really began in the movement in the first four centuries outward from Judea and then throughout the Roman Empire, resulting in its substantial Christianization. For the remainder of the first millennium, missionary growth occurred among the northern barbarians—Goths, Germans, Norsemen—and also among eastern Slavs. The missionary impulse was powerfully present in the movement of the European empires, especially the Spanish and the Portuguese in the sixteenth century, and also in Protestant Christianity, particularly in the nineteenth century. It is still present in many parts of the world. Probably the most significant areas of missionary growth today are Africa, which is also a growth area for Islam, and Eastern Asia, where the substantial Christianization of Korea and very rapid church growth in China are signs that the balance in the distribution of Christians around the world is changing and will continue to change over the next few generations.

For Christians who have come to expect continuing missionary growth around the world in line with the Great Commission, it is hard to come to terms with the loss of areas where Christianity was once strongly established. The two most significant areas in this regard are the Middle East and Western Europe. The Middle East was the original home of Christianity but is now predominantly Islamic. In Western Europe, Christianity's dominant position has to a large extent been replaced by forms of secularism with their own missionary impulse and the outreach of the Christian churches is in some respects surpassed by that of multinational corporations. Two final features of the history of Christian mission also deserve to be noted. First, it has to be acknowledged that, while they are far from identical, there have been strong connections between mission and imperialism. Second, the Christian message has had a persistent appeal to women. The study of the spread of Christianity in new areas very often reveals the importance of its attractiveness to women and the opportunities that it opens up for them for spiritual fulfillment and self-expression, particularly in more oppressive societies.

1.6 Revelation in the Qur'ān
Qur'ān 6:91–92; 25:32; 21:107; 38:87; 33:40

ASMA AFSARUDDIN

6:91–92[1]

[91]They did not estimate God with a true estimation, when they said that God had not revealed anything to humans. Say: "Who then revealed the Book which Moses brought as a light and guidance to humankind, which they render as mere sheets of paper, and of which they expose part and conceal much? [But] you were taught what you and your fathers did not know." Say: "[It is] God"; then leave them to engage in their frivolous conversations. [92]This is a blessed Scripture that We have caused to come down confirming what was before it, so that you may warn the mother of the cities and those around it. And those who believe in the hereafter believe in it and they are vigilant in their prayers.

25:32

[32]Those who disbelieve say, "If only the Qur'ān had been revealed to him as a whole!" But that is how we strengthen your heart by it and reveal it gradually.

21:107

[107]We have not sent you except as a mercy to all people (lit. the worlds).

38:87

[87]It [the Qur'ān] is only a reminder for all people.

33:40

[40]Muhammad is not the father of any of the men among you; rather he is the Messenger of God and the Seal of the Prophets. And God is knowledgeable of everything.

The hermeneutic arenas delineated by the concepts of "finality," "particularity," and "universality" of divine revelation within Islam are rich and complex, and invite deep reflection. Given the constraints of length, this chapter

44

will selectively discuss the meanings of the key verses in the Qur'ān printed above that deal with these concepts as refracted through the perspectives of some of the most important classical exegetes in Islam. The article will then conclude by comparing and assessing these varied perspectives through time and dwell on what insights we may draw from these works and their implications for interfaith conversations among contemporary religious scholars and practitioners.

Qur'ān 6:91–92

The early fourth/tenth-century commentator al-Tabari (d. 310/923) indicates that shifting, multiple audiences are being addressed in these two verses; identification of their audiences is therefore crucial to the exegesis of the verses. He also indicates that the exegetes before and during his time are not in agreement regarding these specific audiences. According to a number of exegetes, the first part of Qur'ān 6:91 could either be addressed to the Jews as a whole in Medina, or to one specific Jewish man, either a certain Malik b. al-Sayf or Fanhas, or, according to another group of exegetes, it could be addressed to the pagan Quraysh (*mushrikū Quraysh*).[2] Al-Tabari prefers the latter view as more appropriate because, he says, the Jews are accustomed to refer to "the scrolls of Abraham and Moses, and the Psalms of David" and therefore would not have denied the fact of divine revelation. On the basis of both reports and/or reason, says al-Tabari, this verse is better understood as referring to the polytheists. The verb *taj'alūna* ("you have rendered"), which indicates direct address to the Jews in this verse, should thus preferably be read as *yaj'alūna* ("they have rendered"), so that the first imperative *qul* ("say") signifies the beginning of a statement directed at the Meccan polytheists alone, in which the Jews are referred to in absentia.[3]

The part of the verse beginning "You were taught" signifies a major shift in the intended audience and redirects divine speech to the believers (*al-mu'minūn*), who have been instructed in much that was previously unknown to them or to their ancestors. Another shift in audience is then immediately indicated by the second *qul* that is directed at the Prophet alone, commanding him to leave aside the pagan Meccans and their foolish talk.[4]

In these shifting, variegated audiences, we have an interplay between particularity and universality. On the one hand, these two verses are firmly anchored in discrete historical moments and address specific individuals and/or groups of people. On the other hand, the particularity of parts of these verses is mitigated by a broader universality undergirding them. This is underscored by al-Tabari when he understands Qur'ān 6:91 as containing a reference to the Jews as having proclaimed the contents of the Torah (*aẓharū min al-tawrā*) but also faulted for, as he comments, "suppressing the mention of Muhammad, peace and blessings be upon him, and what was revealed to him."[5] According to al-Tabari, implicit in this part of the verse is criticism of the Jews for concealing the possibility of continuing revelation after Moses and thus the continuation of God's guidance to all of humankind. The verse is also critical of the desire of the Jews to maintain the particularity of their revelation and rejecting universality by obscuring its organic connection with Islam, which followed in its wake. The Qur'ān undermines this Jewish preference for particularity by confirming in this verse the guidance and enlightenment contained in previous revelations and asserting its own connectedness with them.

But one may ask, might not the rest of Qur'ān 6:92 be understood in a particularist vein since it appears to be restricting the role of the Prophet Muhammad as a warner primarily to "the Mother of Cities and all around it"? Al-Tabari records, however, that the majority of the exegetes were of the opinion that the phrase *wa-li-tundhira umm al-qurā wa-man ḥawlahā* referred to Mecca and what was around it "to the East and the West" (*sharqan wa-gharban*). This is of course a merismic expression that means "everywhere."[6] In fact, a report preserved from Ibn 'Abbas expressly glosses "all around it" as "the entire earth" (*al-arḍ kullahā*).[7]

The sixth/twelfth century rationalist (Muʿtazili) commentator al-Zamakhshari (d. ca. 538/1144) similarly indicates shifting audiences within the two verses and the differences of opinion among the exegetes concerning who exactly was being addressed in these two verses, alternating between the Jews and the Quraysh of Medina. Al-Zamakhshari infers from these verses an implied contrast between the purity, integrity, and finality of the Qur'ān compared to the Torah, which was a source of guidance and illumination in the hands of Moses. However, his later followers "changed it, diminished it, and made it into separate sheets of papers" so that they could display part of it and hide part of it. Like the original Torah vouchsafed to Moses, the Qur'ān revealed to Muhammad is a blessed Book, confirming "what preceded it of scriptures and warnings." *Umm al-qurā*, according to al-Zamakhshari, is a clear reference to Mecca, since it is the "place of the first House created for humankind." Interestingly, he also claims that Mecca is the direction of prayer (*qibla*) for all the people of the *qurā*, which would appear to include non-Muslims as well, and the destination of their pilgrimage, as well as being the most important city among its neighbors.[8] Although this is not explicitly stated, al-Zamakhshari clearly attributes universality to Mecca on account of the Ka'ba that is situated within it and that is associated with Abraham, the pivotal figure in the three Abrahamic religions. Like al-Tabari before him, he too thereby underscores the universality as well as the finality of the Qur'ānic message, rooted as it is in the Abrahamic tradition, which provides the common link with previous monotheistic revelations.

The well-known exegete of the late sixth/twelfth century, Fakhr al-Din al-Razi (d. 606/1210), similarly affirms this understanding and comments that "the Mother of Cities and all around it" is the equivalent of the phrase *kulla al-'ālamīn* (literally "all the worlds").[9] In this understanding, Mecca is the *omphalos* of the earth—the center of human religious consciousness, faith, and praxis—and is not merely associated with the early prophetic career of Muhammad. Thus what appears at first glance to be particular and historically restricted in the verse's reference to the "Mother of Cities" is generally understood by the classical exegetes as confirming rather than undermining the universality of the message of Islam.

Qur'ān 25:32

In his brief commentary on Qur'ān 25:32, al-Tabari records the views of a number of exegetes who affirm that this verse establishes the gradual, progressive nature of the Qur'ānic revelation in the course of over twenty years, so that it could be responsive to specific questions asked by people over time. The word *tartīl* ("gradual revelation") is understood to imply both gradualness and precision in reading/recitation. According to other authorities, among them 'Abd al-Rahman ibn Zayd (d. 182/798),[10] *tartīl* is glossed as "elucidation and explanation or commentary" (*al-tabyīn wa 'l-tafsīr*). This view stresses the simultaneity of exegesis inherent in the act of recitation or reading itself and the importance of measured and deliberate reflection on the word of God, thus establishing a protocol for engaging scripture.[11]

Al-Zamakhshari comments that in contrast to the three previous scriptures (the Torah, the Psalms, and the Gospel, according to Muslim belief) that came down all at once, the Qur'ān was revealed piecemeal over a period of time. Either the Quraysh or the Jews of Medina may have uttered this statement. Al-Zamakhshari says that it would have made no difference to the Qur'ān's inimitable nature or its cogency as a divine proof-text whether it came down all at once or *seriatim*. It was preferable, however, for the Qur'ān to come down gradually, he says, because it allowed the Prophet to memorize it more easily, particularly since, unlike the previous messengers, he could neither read nor write. Like al-Tabari, al-Zamakhshari also emphasizes that the piecemeal revelation of the Qur'ānic verses allowed the Qur'ān to be responsive to specific historical circumstances and to the concerns of the believers, as well as allowing for the possibility of abrogation.[12]

Al-Razi similarly gives several reasons for the gradual revelation of the Qur'ān, one of which is that since Muhammad could not read nor write, this manner of oral revelation was conducive to memorization and allowed for accurate preservation by the Prophet. This is in contrast to the written Torah that could be transmitted all at once and that the literate Moses could read. Another reason is that if the Qur'ān had been revealed all at once, says al-Razi, then the entire divine law would have been imposed immediately on humans, which would have represented an unusual hardship on them.[13]

In their understanding of this verse, our classical exegetes read particularity and singularity into the mode of the revelation of the Qur'ān—its piecemeal nature and groundedness in specific historical circumstances—but at the same time affirm the finality of the Qur'ānic message and its comprehensiveness. Al-Razi in particular emphasizes that revelation is an act of mercy from God, not an imposition on human beings. As such, He facilitates human receptivity toward it and fosters its understanding, the achievement of which represents the highest purpose of humankind. This again is a testament to the universality of the Qur'ānic message because it conforms to the human ability to understand and implement it everywhere and at any time.

Qur'ān 21:107

The description of the Prophet "as a mercy" (*raḥmatan*) in Qur'ān 21:107 is taken as self-explanatory by al-Tabari and receives little comment.[14] But al-Tabari indicates that the exegetes differed among themselves regarding the meaning of *li-'l-'ālamīn* (in our translation "to all people"). Some questioned whether Muhammad had been sent to both the believers and the unbelievers while others, like Ibn 'Abbas, asserted that indeed it was so. 'Abd al-Rahman ibn Zayd, however, had maintained that *al-'ālamūna* referred only to "those who believed in him [the Prophet] and deemed his message true." Al-Tabari regards Ibn 'Abbas' exegesis as more plausible and comments that the Prophet Muhammad was a mercy to both the believers and the unbelievers. In the first instance, the believers were guided to faith and righteous action through the Prophet while in the second, the unbelievers, through his presence among them, were given a reprieve from the divine punishment that had befallen other nations before them.[15] In Ibn 'Abbas' and Ibn Zayd's differing interpretations, we see particularity vying with universality in defining the scope and effect of the prophetic mission of Muhammad. While Ibn Zayd would restrict accessibility to the divine message conveyed by Muhammad to the salvific community of Muslims alone, Ibn 'Abbas' interpretation universalizes access to the same message, whose language and content cut across self-consciously erected confessional boundaries and speak, as we might put it today, to a globalizing world.

Al-Zamakhshari takes it to be self-evident that Muhammad was sent as a mercy to all people, Muslim and non-Muslim, good and bad. In his brief commentary on this verse, al-Zamakhshari maintains that the Prophet came equally to those who followed him willingly, and thereby achieved happiness, and to those who opposed him and refused to follow him, thereby ruining themselves in the process. In other words, everyone potentially had equal access to Muhammad or, conversely, the Prophet made himself available to all. The people around him derived benefit—or not—from his presence and his message, according to their individual choices and actions. To better illustrate what he means, al-Zamakhshari uses the example of a gushing spring that God has caused to spring forth and that is accessible to all. Some people use the water from this spring to irrigate their lands and water their livestock and thus prosper. Others fail to use the spring to water their lands and face financial loss. Despite these different consequences, says al-Zamakhshari, the spring *qua* spring represents a blessing from God and a mercy to both groups of people. Idle people (*al-kaslān*), he says, are a trial to themselves since they willfully deprive themselves of a beneficial thing. Muhammad is a source of mercy even to the morally reprobate (*al-fujjār*), he stresses, because their punishment is averted by his presence in their midst and he grants them protection from being destroyed.[16]

Al-Razi comments extensively on how and why the Prophet Muhammad constituted, as he phrases it, "a mercy in religion and in the world." In brief, al-Razi comments that at the time of his prophetic mission, the people in general lived in ignorance and error, and even the People of the Book were in despair and divided among themselves. Muhammad summoned the people to the truth, showed them the path of salvation, and promulgated laws that clearly distinguished between what is licit and illicit. Although prior nations were destroyed for refusing to obey their prophets, al-Razi references another verse, Qur'an 8:33, that states, "God would not punish them while you [i.e. the Prophet] are among them." Like his predecessors, al-Razi therefore stresses that the Prophet's presence among the unbelievers had warded off divine retribution against them. Like al-Tabari, al-Razi disagrees with Ibn Zayd that the Prophet was sent as a mercy only to the believers and affirms instead that his mercy extended to all. He cites a ḥadīth related by Abu Hurayra in which he [Abu Hurayra] implores Muhammad to inveigh against the polytheists, but the Prophet replies, "Indeed I was sent as a [source of] mercy and not as [a source of] affliction."[17] In the discussion of all three exegetes, mercy and compassion render Muhammad's mission and legacy eminently pleasing and accessible to all and endow them with an enduring universality, triumphing over the parochialism of his own time and place, and those of subsequent generations.

Qur'ān 38:87

The universal significance of the Qur'ān finds quintessential expression in this verse, in which it is described as "only a reminder for all creation." In his very brief commentary on this verse, al-Tabari remarks that the Prophet was asked to assert before the Meccan polytheists that the Qur'ān was a reminder from God and that "all creation" referred to humans and the jinn, who by virtue of their faith could save themselves from perdition.[18]

In his even briefer commentary, al-Zamakhshari simply says that the verse refers to the Qur'ān as a reminder from God and refers to the twin realms of humans and the jinn.[19]

Al-Razi understands *dhikr* in relation to the Qur'ān as that which prompts "every sound mind and upright disposition" to attest to the truth and majesty of the divine law (*al-sharī'a*) and to avoid what is false and corrupt.[20] This verse has a variant in Qur'ān 6:90, where the Qur'ān is described as "a reminder to all creation," which al-Razi understands to be an affirmation that Muhammad was "sent to all the people of the world" and not to any specific group of people to the exception of others.[21]

Qur'ān 33:40

With regard to this final verse, al-Tabari, al-Zamakhshari, and al-Razi all understand the phrase "the seal of the prophets" (*khatam al-nabīyīn*) to be fairly self-explanatory in referring to the finality of Muhammad's prophethood and the cessation of direct revelation from God after him.[22] Al-Zamakhshari adds that the verse also underscores that Muhammad had no male progeny who, on reaching adulthood, would also have become a prophet, as apparently Muhammad himself had remarked when his infant son Ibrahim died.[23] Al-Zamakhshari goes on to entertain a possible question in this context: since Jesus was going to come at the end of time, how can one say that Muhammad was the last prophet? The answer is, al-Zamakhshari says, that no one else after Muhammad will function as a prophet. Although Jesus was a prophet before Muhammad, when he returns he will return as one who practices the sharī'a of Muhammad and who will pray toward his *qibla* as a member of his community.[24] Clearly in al-Zamakhshari's conceptualization, the finality of Islam dissolves the particularities of previous revelations and, at the end of time, only the universal divine law as embodied in the sharī'a of Islam will prevail.

Al-Razi also adds that one who is the last of all prophets is particularly compassionate toward his community and is the most excellent guide for it, just like the father who is especially solicitous toward his only son. A prophet who knows there will be someone to succeed him is not perhaps as punctilious in conveying his message for he knows that his successor will be able to make up for his lapses.[25] The clear implication is that Muhammad as the last of a long line of prophets did not have the luxury of making any mistakes, as did his predecessors, ensuring the finality and completeness of his message for all of humankind.

Conclusion

Taken together, the verses discussed above indicate that although the meanings of some of them may be circumscribed by discrete historical circumstances, fully acknowledged by our exegetes, there is a larger universality that runs as a common thread through all of them. Furthermore, the mechanics of revelation are understood to be historically determined but the overall Qur'ānic message itself is final, eternal, and universal. Thus, our exegetes affirm, the Qur'ān was revealed piecemeal because of the contingent fact that Muhammad was unlettered, that it was initially an oral transmission, and that the sharī'a—on account of its comprehensiveness—could not be revealed in its entirety at any one time. In contrast, the Torah was revealed in written form and received all at once by Moses who was literate. Implicit in this contrast (it is not explicitly stated in the exegeses we surveyed) is also the assumption that the Torah, described as a source of guidance for humanity, is not as comprehensive as the Qur'ān and awaited finality and full realization in the prophethood of Muhammad, a fact believed to have been already foreshadowed in the text of the Torah itself. Exegeses of *tartīl* suggest that although direct divine revelation to humans ceased after the revelation of the Qur'ān, whose text is final and unchanging, the process of elucidation and exegesis allows multiple layers of meaning of the text to emerge over time. The Qur'ān in interaction with its reader/audience remains a dynamic "lived" text. Therefore, its finality is open-ended rather than closed. The possibility of continuing to uncover multiple meanings within the Qur'ānic text in varying historical circumstances confers upon it semantic and contextual pluralism, thus rendering it beyond the bounds of human time and place— hence, truly universal.

In the Qur'ānic context, finality transcends particularity. Thus the finality of Muhammad's status as "the seal of the prophets" is yet grounded in universality, which the Qur'ān underscores by directing the apostolic message to all the world and its peoples. This may be assumed to be in contrast to the particularity of the Torah that had restricted its message to the Hebrew people. This overwhelming sense of the particularity blending into the universality of the message of Islam leads to the uniform exegesis of 6:92 ("the Mother of cities and all around it") as a reference to both Mecca and the wide world beyond it. There may be a possible connection between *umm al-qurā*, "the mother of cities" and *umm al-kitāb* (43:4) "the mother of the Book," the heavenly prototype of God's complete revelation. The term *umm* in both these phrases potentially links authenticity and incorruptibility to universality.

Universality is furthermore predicated on mercy and remembrance of God. The description of Muhammad as "mercy to the peoples" and the description of the Qur'ān as "a reminder to all peoples" are complementary and all-enveloping. The Arabic word *al-'ālamīn* is too capacious to be expressed by a single English word. It is literally "worlds" and encompasses not only all realms, worldly and otherworldly, but all species of beings, humans, and jinns. A concordance of the Qur'ān lists 73 occurrences of the term *al-'ālamīn*. Clearly, in the Qur'ānic repertoire, this is a significant term whereby the Qur'ān lays claim to a universality the scope of which defies adequate human comprehension and transcends worldly spatial categories.

Al-Zamakhshari's cooptation of the eschatological Christ, who, according to al-Zamakshshari, will return as a confessional Muslim at the end of time, potentially has important implications for Christian-Muslim relations. In this particular exegesis, all three elements—particularity, finality, and universality—are in play and each one could be understood to be ascendant. In asserting that Jesus will specifically adopt the law of Muhammad and pray in the direction of the Ka'ba, al-Zamakhshari is clearly articulating a triumphalist, particularist understanding of the salvific efficacy of Islam alone. Such a statement is not to be found in the Qur'ān but it does occur in some ḥadīth collections. Al-Zamakhshari is also categorically proclaiming the finality of Muhammad's message and Islam's supersession of the other Abrahamic faiths. Even though such a position goes against the Qur'ānic view that its revelation confirms (*muṣaddiq*) rather than abrogates or supersedes previous revelations, it has become quite prevalent. At the same time, al-Zamakhshari is also affirming that Islam is a universal and universalizing faith, strikingly encoded in Jesus's formal embrace and recognition of Islam as the true eschatological religion, the one and only that endures the vicissitudes of time to triumph over all falsehood and deception in the end. While confessional Christianity was valid in its own time and place, it was meant to reach its revelatory apotheosis in the universalizing crucible of Islam. These views of al-Zamakhshari are not unknown among Muslims in general and are often tied to the pious hope that well-meaning Christians will discover this for themselves.

Scriptural exegesis thus poses a challenge for both Muslims and Christians, as for others. Both communities have read their sacred texts in exclusivist and inclusivist ways. Our selective survey of classical exegetical texts demonstrates that Muslim Qur'ān-commentators have read a variety of meanings into the Qur'ānic text and their motives for doing so were often conditioned by historical circumstances and individual proclivities, a full discussion of which would not be possible here. Ultimately, these multiple readings were engendered by a constant negotiation between particularity/ies and universality/ies, mediated by notions of what represents the final and absolute truth. Such a process of negotiation continues unabated today and continues to have especially important implications for the relations of Muslims with Christians.

Notes

1. All translations from the Qur'ān, including those at the beginning of the paper, are mine.
2. Al-Tabari, *Tafsīr al-Ṭabarī called Jāmi' al-bayān fī ta'wīl al-Qur'ān* (Beirut, 1997), 5:264 ff.
3. Ibid., 5:265.
4. Ibid., 5:265–66.
5. Ibid., 5:265.
6. A *merism* is a figure of speech in which the extremes of a category are mentioned in order to indicate its totality. "They searched high and low," meaning "they searched everywhere," is an example in English of such a merismic expression.
7. Ibid., 5:267.
8. Al-Zamakhshari, *al-Kashshāf 'an ḥaqā'iq ghawāmiḍ al-tanzīl wa-'uyūn al-aqāwīl fī wujūh al-ta'wīl*, eds. 'Adil Ahmad 'Abd al-Mawjud and 'Ali Muhammad Mu'awwid (Riyadh, 1998), 2:370–71.
9. Al-Razi, *al-Tafsīr al-kabīr* (Beirut, 1999), 5:65.
10. This is the Successor 'Abd al-Rahman Ibn Zayd b. Aslam al-'Adawi al-Madani, son of the well-known Companion Zayd b. Aslam, from whom the former transmitted ḥadīths. Ibn Zayd was known to have composed a Qur'ān commentary that was used by al-Tabari, as well as a work titled *Kitāb al-nāsikh wa-'l-mansūkh*; cf. Fuat Sezgin, *Geschichte des Arabischen Schrifttums* (Leiden, 1967), 1:38.
11. Al-Tabari, *Tafsīr*, 9:387.
12. Al-Zamakhshari, *Kashshāf*, 4:347–48.
13. Al-Razi, *Tafsīr*, 8:457.
14. Al-Tabari, *Tafsīr*, 9:100.
15. Ibid., 9:101.
16. Al-Zamakhshari, *Kashshāf*, 4:170.
17. Al-Razi, *Tafsīr*, 8:193.
18. Al-Tabari, *Tafsīr*, 10:608.
19. Al-Zamakhshari, *Kashshāf*, 5:285.
20. Al-Razi, *Tafsīr*, 9:416–17.

21. Ibid., 5:58.

22. Al-Tabari, *Tafsīr*, 10:305; al-Zamakhshari, *Kashshāf*, 5:76; al-Razi, *Tafsīr*, 9:171.

23. Al-Zamakhshari, *Kashshāf*, 5:75. The editor points out that this report is preserved by Ibn Maja in his *Sunan* in the section on "al-janā'iz."

24. Al-Zamakhshari, *Kashshāf*, 5:76.

25. Al-Razi, *Tafsīr*, 9:171.

PART II

Translating the Word?

2.1 Translating the Qur'ān

MUHAMMAD ABDEL HALEEM

The Qur'ān was revealed at a particular time in a particular locality and in a particular language but it states that its message was intended to be universal, for all places and times (25:1; 34:28). However, two factors have made the process of communicating the message to non-Arabs complex: first, the conviction on the part of the faithful that the text is the divine word, that God Himself is the speaker throughout; second, the fact that, in several places in the Qur'ān, it is described as being Arabic (*innā anzalnāhu Qur'ānan 'arabīyan*, 12:2).[1] The significance and implications of the way these statements have been understood by successive generations of Muslim scholars would prove crucial in discussing the way it should be communicated to non-Arabs.

The first question that comes to mind is, "Why was this issue of language raised at all in the Qur'ān?" There were two reasons for this: the first is that Muhammad, the recipient of the revelation of the Qur'ān, was an Arab, preaching the message to Arabs as one of them. "It was He [God] who raised a messenger among the *ummiyīn* [people who had no scripture] to recite His revelation to them, to make them grow spiritually and to teach them the scripture and wisdom—before that they were clearly astray—to them and others yet to follow them" (62:2–3). Muhammad was the first messenger and the Qur'ān the first scripture that the Arabs in Mecca had received. Like all messages, the Qur'ān had to be in the language of the people: "We have never sent a messenger who did not use his own people's language to make things clear to them" (14:4). So, very early in his message, God tells Muhammad, "Warn your nearest kinsfolk" (26:214). Then he is told, "We have revealed to you an Arabic Qur'ān in order that you may warn the capital town [Mecca] and all who live nearby" (42:7).

The second reason, which the Qur'ān stresses in several places, is that it is revealed to them in Arabic so that they may understand (12:2) and have no excuse, just as it gives all varieties of explanations and arguments so that they may understand and have no excuse (6:65–66).

59

The natural description of the Qur'ān as being in Arabic could not have been intended to mean, as some jurists came to think, that it should not be translated nor, as Shafi'i (d. 204/820) asserted, clearly on the basis of the Arabic Qur'ān being the word of God, that just as followers of all earlier religions had to give up their religion and become Muslims, they had to follow the Prophet's language and learn from it as much as they could of the prayers and other requirements of the faith.[2]

An Early Example of Translation

During the early years of the Prophet's life he was addressing the Arabs, with a few non-Arab individuals like Bilal the Abyssinian, Salman the Persian, and Suhaib the Roman, who had been living in Arabia and were conversant with the Arabic language. There was no need for the Prophet, being so busy with the Arabs, to think how his universal message was to be communicated to non-Arabs. After the conquest of Mecca and the spread of Islam throughout Arabia, he began to think of communicating the word beyond its borders. He sent letters to the important neighboring rulers of that time, the Emperor of Byzantium, the King of Persia, the King of Ethiopia, and the Patriarch of Alexandria, inviting them to embrace Islam.[3] These letters contained a number of Qur'ānic verses, including 3:64 and 59:22–24. It was taken for granted by the Prophet and the people around him that the recipients would not know Arabic and that the content, including the Qur'ānic verses, would have to be translated for them, even though he knew very well that, in Arabic, the Qur'ān challenged the Arabs themselves to produce anything equal to it. Clearly the Prophet considered that translation was a suitable means of communication. We are told in the biographical books (sīra) that the letters and the verses were translated for the recipients so that they could understand. This is clear endorsement of the necessity and permissibility of translating the scripture. One wonders: If any of the foreign leaders had answered favorably and become a Muslim, are we to assume that the Prophet would have expected him to pray in Arabic the next day? The Prophet was known for making things easy for people, and did not even insist that the different tribes of Arabia should pronounce the Qur'ān's words according to the pronunciation of the Quraysh dialect he himself used, rather than their own. Such latitude was not to be emulated by later generations of Muslim scholars and this has implications for all non-Arab Muslims.

The Growing Need for Translation and Discussion of Its Limits

Soon after the Prophet, Arab Muslims spread beyond Arabia at a remarkable speed and people in different countries began, no doubt gradually, to accept the new faith. Becoming a Muslim in itself does not require knowledge of the Qur'ān or Arabic, but it is a requirement of the five daily prayers to recite the first short chapter of the Qur'ān (al-Fātiḥa). The question of reading the Fātiḥa in prayer was soon to be discussed by the early jurists. Abu Hanifa, who was born eighty-one years after the Hijra and who was descended from a Persian family, is reported to have said that Persian Muslims who could not read Arabic could read the Fātiḥa in their own language. It is reported that two of his jurist colleagues differed from his view and that eventually he himself changed his mind. Abu Hanifa and the Hanafi scholars who later adopted his view rely, for the permissibility of translation, on the Prophet's letters to foreign leaders and on the fact that the Qur'ān speaks of its message as being in the earlier scriptures, which means that Arabic is not an inseparable part of its meaning. The Qur'ānic verse, "God does not burden any soul with more than it can bear" (2:86) is also invoked. However, Shafi'i, a Qurayshi Arab, rejected this view, saying that if a Muslim cannot read the Fātiḥa in Arabic, he should merely glorify God in his own language. Because the Qur'ān was revealed in Arabic, and it was inimitable in Arabic, if it were translated into any other language this inimitability would cease.[4] Maliki, Hanbali, and Zahiri scholars also held the view that reading translations of the Qur'ān in the prayer is inadmissible. Ibn Hazm (d. 456/1064) considered it ḥaram (forbidden) to read a translation of the Fātiḥa or any other Qur'ānic passage in the prayer but he conceded that it was permissible to recite supplication and glorification of God in other languages. The flexibility and desire to make things easy shown by the Prophet was unfortunately not followed by the jurists; in fact, they made things difficult. But they allowed the use of translation in the sense of interpreting the meaning or tafsīr outside the prayer in order to make it easier for people to understand the Qur'ān.

The Arabic of the Qur'ān was recognized by Arabs, Muslims, and non-Muslims to be of surpassing eloquence and this became the view of non-Arab Muslim scholars, who played a major role in codifying the grammar of the Arabic language, the science of rhetoric in Arabic, and indeed the interpretation of the Qur'ān. It was these people who, no less than Arabs, vehemently defended the eloquence of the Qur'ān and insisted that it could not be translated. Al-Jahiz (d. 255/869) considered that excellence in poetry was confined to the genius of the Arabs, and anyone who spoke Arabic, and that Arabic poetry could not be translated, let alone the Qur'ān, which was more difficult and hazardous to translate. The Ikhwan al-Safa, a group of Arab and non-Arab philosophers, theologians, and intellectuals who flourished in Basra in the fourth/tenth century, again said that no one from any nation, with all their various languages, could translate the Qur'ān from Arabic into any other language.[5] The stylistic features of the Qur'ān were seen to be too complex and elusive for anyone to try to translate into another language without massive loss. This awe felt by the Muslims, Arabs and non-Arabs toward the eloquence of the Qur'ānic language has continued to be a crucial factor in the issue of the translation of the Qur'ān.

Scholars like Jahiz, who held the view that Arabic poetry was superior to the poetry of other languages and that translating it made it lose its distinction, would naturally consider that Arabic was the most fitting language for the Qur'ān. However, what is certain is the distinction that the Qur'ān conferred on the Arabic language. The effect of the Qur'ān on Arabic was dramatic, profound, and lasting, to an extent unknown in any other language. It was the Qur'ān that took Arabic outside Arabia to become a lingua franca for what is now the whole Arab world, and the religious lingua franca for the whole Muslim world. It was adopted by people in the Fertile Crescent, North Africa, and then even Persia, superseding such local languages as Aramaic, Greek, Coptic, Berber, and Persian. In Persia it became the language of administration, literature, and religion for some centuries.

As more non-Arabs embraced Islam, the need arose for explanation of the Arabic language. Arabic grammar and phonetics were codified, the Arabic script developed into fine calligraphy, and the study of Arabic rhetoric developed in order to identify the stylistic features that make up the language of the Qur'ān. Non-Arab Muslim scholars played a major role in all this.

Although scholars held that the Qur'ān is untranslatable, whether because of it being the word of God, because it stressed that it was an "Arabic Qur'ān," or because of the rich stylistic features of the language, they were aware that the message of Islam had to be communicated to non-Arabs. In the first instance this was done orally. Jahiz reports a specific preacher of his time, who was equally eloquent in Arabic and Persian. He would sit with Arabs on his right and Persians on his left and read a verse in Arabic, explain its meaning for

Arabs in Arabic, then turn to the Persians and explain its meaning for them in Persian. No one could determine in which language he was more eloquent.[6] This oral method of explaining the Qur'ān to non-Arabs was reported in different parts of the Muslim world, in Africa and Asia.

As regards written translations, when the Samanid ruler of Persia, Mansur Ibn Nuh (reigned 961–76 CE) reinstated Persian as the national language, he decided on translating Tabari's *tafsīr*. A forty-volume copy was brought from Baghdad and he commissioned a large number of scholars who made an abridged translation of about ten volumes into Persian to be interwoven line by line with the Arabic text of the Qur'ān, setting a tradition that has continued to the present.

There are historical reports from the fifth Hijra century and from Zamakhshari in the sixth century that show that there were translations, in the sense of *tafsīr*, in every non-Arab Muslim nation and that this was the medium of communicating the Qur'ān and its teachings.[7] Shatibi in the eighth century states that translation, in the sense of *tafsīr*, was used to make the text accessible to people just as *tafsīr* was used in the Arab lands to make the Qur'ān accessible to the masses.[8]

Bilingual editions giving the different languages on alternate lines can be seen in many old manuscripts and printed books from Asia, Africa, and even Europe in the British Museum and elsewhere. The first printed translation, titled *tafsīr al-Qur'ān*, was published in Istanbul in 1826. Printed translations followed in other Islamic languages, all of them being called *tarjama tafsīriyya* (explanatory translations). The Arabic texts were printed in a larger font than the *tarjama tafsīriyya*, which were on alternate lines. In the mosques of London one can see copies of the Qur'ān printed in Pakistan in the same fashion adopted centuries earlier, with Urdu lines alternating with the Arabic. More recently the convention has been to have facing pages in the two languages, parallel columns, or with translation surrounding the Arabic text.

On the whole, Muslims have remained faithful to the ideas that the Qur'ān has to remain in Arabic and that it is untranslatable. Any translation is thus not the Qur'ān; it is no more than an interpretation or *tafsīr* and it is not admissible to deduce judicial rulings (fatwās) from a translation. However, the twentieth century brought momentous events: the Caliphate was abolished in Turkey and a ban was imposed on using Arabic script. The discussion on the permissibility of translating the Qur'ān and using non-Arabic languages for prayer was reopened. Support for this was sought from the Hanafi school of law and it was argued that the linguistic barrier between the ordinary Muslims and the text of the Qur'ān should be removed. The discussions that followed in Egypt were crucial. A fatwā, issued in 1936, allowed the possibility of interpretative translation or translating the meaning of the Qur'ān, but also emphasized the impossibility of translating the words.[9] In the opinion of the Rector of Al-Azhar at that time, Shaikh M. Mustafa al-Maraghi, prayer could be performed in languages other than Arabic and judicial rulings could be deduced from translations since they were normally deduced from the meanings of the Arabic words. Marmaduke Pickthall, who happened to consult scholars from Al-Azhar around that time, called his translation *The Meaning of the Glorious Qur'ān: An Explanatory Translation* and Muslim translators normally followed this convention. Muslims still do not regard translations as the Qur'ān.

Many Muslim governments now insist on Arabic being included with any translation before they allow copies to be circulated for sale. Having Arabic in bilingual editions provides the reference against which any translation is checked and guards the Qur'ān itself from adulteration. Far from being seen as a stumbling block or a barrier, the existence of the Qur'ān in Arabic and including it with translations is thus considered an advantage.

This concern on the part of Muslims needs to be seen in the context of the history of translations of the Qur'ān by Western scholars. Whereas well-known translations of the Bible, such as the Authorized Version or the Revised Standard Version, were produced by groups of believing scholars working in their own language with full knowledge of the Bible and high command of English and other languages, the situation with the translation of the Qur'ān in the West was quite different. The Qur'ān was first translated into Latin as part of the "war of the spirit," rather than the "war of the sword" during the Crusades, and for centuries refutation and denigration were explicit aims of the study and translation of the Qur'ān.[10] Moreover, translation was left to individuals, some of whose command of Arabic ranged from nonexistent to questionable, to say the least. This situation changed dramatically later on, culminating in the work of Arberry, who, with his command of Arabic and respect for the Qur'ān, stands as the finest example. The history of hostile translations is the reason why Muslims, both in the West and in Muslim countries, do not trust translations made by non-Muslims and why translations by Muslims such as Pickthall and Yusuf Ali have reigned supreme among Muslims for a long time. Recently, we have witnessed the rush by publishers to cash in on the market, with various individual translators producing versions of the Qur'ān for them. Since 9/11 more than eight translations have appeared in English. In such an atmosphere, Muslims would not rely on any one translation.

Ṣalāt—Obligatory Prayers

If the Qur'ān has long been seen by Muslims as inseparable from Arabic, it is perhaps surprising that this has also been the case with ṣalāt. We have seen that much of the discussion by jurists centered around whether it was permissible for those who could not read Arabic to read the Fātiḥa in a foreign language during the obligatory prayers. The only part of the prayer that comes directly from the Qur'ān is the Fātiḥa. It is only recommended that another short passage from the Qur'ān should be recited after the Fātiḥa but the prayer is valid without this. Muslims have remained faithful to learning the prayer and performing it in Arabic. This is part of the education of Muslim children. Being the second pillar of Islam and part of every practicing Muslim's daily activity, Arabic prayer must have contributed to people's faithfulness to Arabic. Indeed, the prayer comes down from the teachings and practice of the Prophet himself. The fact that it consists of Arabic words that he uttered gives them a very special status. They have to be learned and repeated in Arabic and this, in any case, is not a difficult task. In fact, the amount of Arabic that has to be learned for the prayer is not that much for a non-Arab to learn. There is the Qur'ānic passage of the Fātiḥa and another passage, tashahhud, at the close of the prayer. Everything else comes in short formulae: allāhu akbar, subḥāna rabbī in the kneeling and prostration positions; sāmiʿ allāhu liman ḥamida when rising from bowing; and the final as-salāmu ʿalaykum twice. These short formulae such as as-salāmu ʿalaykum and allāhu akbar have become part of the daily lives of Muslims and have become known in other languages even to non-Muslims.

It must also be remembered that the influence of Arabic in the languages of Muslim countries has been immense; for example, 60 percent of the Persian vocabulary is still of Arabic origin. The influence of Arabic also applies to languages derived from Persian, like Urdu. Religious vocabulary is naturally central to this process of linguistic influence, which makes the learning and performance of prayer in Arabic much easier. Ṣalāt, with its Arabic formulae, is felt intensely by Muslims, Arabs, and non-Arabs, and recalls for Muslims at any place or time the very words used in prayer by successive generations of Muslims since the Prophet's time. This unites Muslims geographically and historically. Beyond the obligatory Arabic parts of the prayers, it is open for Muslims to include in their own languages whatever personal supplications they wish to make to God. These come before the prayer, in the kneeling and prostration positions, and at the close of the prayers after the *salām*. Thus *ṣalāt* is not a routine or impoverished exercise. This is what has made Muslims stick to Arabic for all the prayers. In fact, prayer makes individual Muslims keen to learn some Arabic. Prayer also remains one of the most unifying factors among Muslims. Wherever Muslims go in the world, they know that they will find other Muslims making exactly the same prayer in the same language. Indeed, a Muslim from any part of the world can lead Arabs in prayer as an imam and is qualified to do so.

To What Extent Did the Insistence on Arabic Affect Communication of the Message of the Qur'ān?

The effect is actually not as one might at first expect. Communication is achieved through *tafsīr* and through the ḥadīth, which confirm what is in the Qur'ān, explaining it or adding information to what is there, in ways that do not contradict the Qur'ān. Ḥadīth literature is much larger than the Qur'ān. Actually *fiqh* (Islamic jurisprudence) relies much more on the ḥadīth than the Qur'ān. It is very striking that despite all the discussions that raged for centuries on the admissibility or possibility of the translation of the Qur'ān, no such discussion took place about the ḥadīth, the *tafsīr*, the biography of the Prophet (*sīra*), or Islamic history. The great works in Arabic on all these subjects have been translated into other languages and have become part of the cultures of Muslims in all their localities. Communication is also achieved through preaching in mosques and elsewhere in local languages. In Britain's mosques, for example, it is true that a sermon is given in Arabic, but additional sermons are given in other languages. *Du'a* (supplications) have a special position, since the Prophet left many *du'a*, which Muslims regularly repeat, and many non-Arab Muslims learn some of them in Arabic. I asked an English convert why she made *du'a* in Arabic rather than in English. She said, "The Arabic words are like a magic formula for me, spoken by the Prophet, and nothing can substitute for them, not even the translations of these *du'a*, which are available in the ḥadīth."

For the masses, translation or *tafsīr* is enough, but in every Muslim country there are specialists who are well versed in Arabic. Indeed all advanced studies on the Qur'ān are done in Arabic or with the Arabic very much in mind. When I see an ayatollah, or a professor of Islamic studies in Indonesia, Malaysia, or Africa, I speak to him in Arabic knowing well that he will understand me and answer me in Arabic because all his advanced studies of the Qur'ān, even in his own country, would have been done in Arabic. Arabic script is still used by speakers of Persian and Urdu (as it used to be by speakers of Malay and Turkish), so those literate in these languages are able to read the Arabic for themselves. Others are now helped by the inclusion in some translations of transliteration in Roman script. This is much sought after and welcomed by many non-Arab Muslims. Individual Muslims feel the need to pronounce the Arabic words even if they do not know their meaning, and consider doing so to be a blessing (*baraka*). Many non-Arab Muslims also make special efforts and take courses to enable them to learn to read and recite the Arabic properly.

Communication of the message of the Qur'ān is achieved by translation, just as it is by the translations of the Bible. As we have seen, translations of the Qur'ān into Muslim languages have existed for centuries, even though they were called *tafsīr*, and they were certainly found adequate for communication of the message. Some might even be of better quality than some translations of the Qur'ān we have in English, bearing in mind that the translators were very good scholars of Arabic, were translating into their own languages, and were fully at home in their knowledge of Islam.

What Muslims call "explanatory translations" or "translations of the meaning" are actually what Westerners understand simply as translations. Indeed, I would say that it may be better to aim for an explanatory translation of the meaning. The oddities we have in many English translations result from excessive literalism, and adherence to the syntactical and stylistic peculiarities of the Arabic language and the language of the Qur'ān, which is very concise, idiomatic, figurative, and elliptical.

Conclusion

In conclusion we can say that the perceived difficulty that non-Arabs encounter with Arabic prayer is highly exaggerated, as is the perception that communication of the Qur'ānic message is hindered by insistence on referring back to the

Arabic Qur'ān. It has also been seen that there is no foundation for thinking that the Qur'ān was not translated from the early centuries of Islam into the various languages and cultures of local Muslims. It is true, of course, that Muslims consider the Arabic text of the Qur'ān untranslatable in the sense that nobody is able to produce a translation of equal literary merit. This is not surprising since the Arabs themselves consider the Arabic Qur'ān inimitable even in Arabic, and nobody has risen to the challenge of producing anything similar to it. This serves to confirm the high esteem in which the Arabic Qur'ān is held and to prompt people to learn it by heart in Arabic and to pronounce the divine words as communicated to and pronounced by the Prophet and all successive generations of Muslims. Every Muslim child, male or female, has to learn some sūras of the Qur'ān in Arabic, and many go on to memorize the whole text. Reading from the Arabic text is a regular act of worship, not only as part of the obligatory prayer but in addition to it. It is part of many rites of passage such as birth, marriage, and death. In this way the original text of the Qur'ān becomes the common property and cultural treasure of all Muslims, not exclusively of scholars of Arabic. They trust the Arabic more than any translation. Learning the Arabic Qur'ān initiates the individual Muslim into the community of all Muslims geographically and historically as they read directly the very words of the message sent down from the Lord of all the Worlds: "This Qur'ān has been sent down from the Lord of the Worlds: the Trustworthy Spirit brought it down to your heart, Prophet, so that you could bring warning, in a clear Arabic tongue. This was foretold in the scriptures of earlier religions" (26:192–96).

Notes

1. M. F. ʿAbdulbaqi lists ten such citations: al-Muʿjam al-mufahras li-alfāẓ al-Qur'ān al karīm (Cairo, 1945, reprinted Beirut, n.d), 456.

2. Muhammad bin Idris al-Shafiʿi, al-Risāla (Cairo, 1983), 29, 31.

3. A. Guillaume, (trans.), The Life of Muhammad: A Translation of Ibn Ishaq's Sīrat Rasūl Allāh (Oxford: Oxford University Press, 1968), 652–59.

4. Shafiʿi's statement is in al-Kasani, Badāʾi al-ṣanāʾi (Cairo, 1327/1909), vol. 1, 112, cited in A. Tibawi, Aḥkām tarjamat al-Qur'ān al-karīm wa taʾrīkhuhā (Beirut, 1979), 7.

5. Rasāʾil ikhwān al-ṣafaʾ (Cairo, 1928), vol. 3, 153, 171, 253.

6. Ismat Binark and Halit Eren, World Bibliography of Translations of the Meanings of the Holy Qur'ān (in English and Arabic), edited with an Arabic introduction by Ekmeleddin

Ihsanoglu (Istanbul: OIC Research Centre for Islamic History, Art and Culture, 1986), xxii (English introduction) and 12 (Arabic introduction).

7. Zamakhshari, cited in Tibawi, *Aḥkām*, 17–18.

8. Tibawi, ibid.

9. On the 1936 fatwā, see Binark and Eren, ed., *World Bibliography*, 15 (Arabic Introduction), and a list of al-Azhar articles referred to on 31. See also M. M. Hussain, *al-Ittijāhāt al-waṭaniyya fi-l-adab al-muʿāṣir* (Cairo, 1984), vol. 2, 312–13.

10. Schweigger's German translation of 1616 and Ross's English translation of 1649 have similar titles associating the "Alcoran of Mahomet" with the Turkish "superstition" or "vanities."

2.2 Translation and the Incarnate Word
Scripture and the Frontier of Languages

LAMIN SANNEH

Translation, Incarnation, and Sacrifice

The case for Bible translation rests squarely on the primacy of divine encounter rather than on claims of cultural advantage. There was long-standing resistance to the principle of vernacular Bible translation because it was feared that would open the scripture to corruption and to unauthorized access, including access by the untutored masses. Opponents argued that already God had at His disposal numerous languages enough for the peoples of the world to make their prayers and worship to need another language, with the suggestion that the limits had been set. That seems unassailable only if you grant the premise that the truth of God would not be diminished by one less translation, by one less national appropriation, making an exclusive *lingua sacra* essential to religious orthodoxy. Furthermore, far from strengthening the church, opponents charged that Bible translation had only stoked the embers of religious strife and division, driving Christians into warring camps. In any event, critics pointed out, had not God remained content by having His name acknowledged as great in Israel and in no other place? In those days, the dew lay on Gideon's fleece only, while the rest of the earth lay dry (Judges 6:36–40). Nothing of that partial bestowal detracted from the omnipotence of God. Accordingly, in spite of the cultural restriction, the singular and generous sovereignty of God was demonstrated for the world to see.[1] Christianity could not forego the idea of a *lingua sacra* without undercutting its claim to truth.

The issue of restricted access to scripture preoccupied Reformation England as it contemplated having the Bible in the national language. Those appointed to the task fussed about whether another translation would be just a labor of debasement fraught with personal peril, or whether it belonged with the deeper question about the history and nature of revelation and, thus, about the future of the church. What kind of merit could another translation claim? And what principle would a fresh translation promote?

To these questions the translators of what came to be called the King James Bible gave both a general and a specific answer, and it would repay us to look closely at their arguments. On the general front, translation was not an exercise in linguistic perfection: you do not justify doing a new translation because of what you consider to be flaws in earlier translations, for you would then be guilty of the charge of the translator as traitor (*traduttore traditore*) and be judged to have impugned the faith of those who came before you. Besides, opinions varied greatly as to what flaws constituted a valid justification for overthrowing a hallowed precedent.[2] "We never thought," the translators declared, "from the beginning that we should need to make a new translation, nor yet to make of a bad one a good one. To that purpose there were many chosen, that were greater in other men's eyes than in their own, and that sought the truth rather than their own praise."[3] Scripture is God's word and not a commodity of national advantage, and so national interest as well as scholarly resources should stand in relation to scripture like the banks to a stream, not to dam but to channel what they encounter. Christianity is a translated religion, and that fact contains at its core the dynamic principle of continuous translatability on account precisely of the fact that God's mind is not closed nor His reach restricted. The multiple languages of a diverse humanity are proof of that. Ultimately, Bible translation is theological in the sense of being a discourse in truth-seeking. Scripture is God's vigil among us.

It is that impulse of open choice that inspired Tyndale, "acknowledged as the most formative influence on the text of the King James Bible," to expand on the theme of popular access in his remarks on the necessity, not just of translation, but of translation in the mother tongue. "If God spare my life," he challenged an opponent in words that eerily smacked of his imminent tragic fate, "ere many years I will cause a boy that driveth the plough shall know more about the Scriptures than thou doest."[4] At stake for Tyndale was a theological principle, though in the circumstances his views carried social and political implications. He expressed himself with unbounded confidence about opening scripture to common access.

Tyndale's confidence was remarkable for its unswerving commitment to the people's natural idiom, for what Archbishop Donald Coggan calls Tyndale's "almost uncanny gift of simplicity . . . a true nobility of homeliness."[5] Tyndale's cause was not alien to Christianity even though he was deemed a heretic for it. The opposition to him proved deadly, but it was not because he was threatening to do a new thing in Christianity altogether but because of the imputation to him of political motives.[6] After all, Tertullian (c.160–c.240), who converted to Christianity in 195, expressed similar views about the Gospel in the languages of the peoples of the world, as did Irenaeus (c.130–c.200), and numerous others after them, including Otfrid von Weissenburg in the ninth century.[7]

It is not merely that the different languages of the world, including English, are an obstacle that the church must overcome to establish the faith, but that in its variety language is a god-given asset, allowing Christianity to invest in language, any language, on the basis that God is to be encountered there. The role assigned to language in the Bible makes language deeply theological, deeply sacramental. As Shakespeare put it, "words without thoughts never to heaven go." It is impossible without language to know and to worship God, or even to have personality, as Diedrich Westermann noted. "By taking away a people's language," he wrote, "we cripple or destroy its soul, and kill its mental individuality."[8] Thomas Huxley defended teaching the Bible in schools in England on the ground that the Bible is necessary to the building of moral character. "By the study of what other book," he asked, "could children be so humanized?"[9] And so the translators affirmed their "desire that the Scripture may speak like itself, as in the language of Canaan, that it may be understood even of the very vulgar."[10] Language as the medium of revelation is Christianity's formative medium.[11] With all its in-built limitation, translation is the imprinting of the divine communication on the rainbow canvas of a rich, diverse humanity. It is that circumstance that emboldened Tyndale, for example, to feel there was nothing new about his wish to translate: God willed it from the beginning. Had God "not made the English tongue? Why forbid ye him to speak in the English tongue then?"[12] It justified instituting English not only in scripture but also in worship.

As Thomas Cranmer (1489–1556) demonstrated, in the end the case for scripture in the "vulgar tongue" was unassailable on the general principle that translation is the original language of religion in Christianity. "There are doubtless many different languages in the world," the Apostle Paul observes, "and none is without meaning; but if I do not know the meaning of the language, I shall be a foreigner to the speaker and the speaker a foreigner to me" (1 Corinthians 14:10–11). Tyndale advanced that view, making him determined to naturalize the gospel in the common idiom. Having laid out the case for the mother tongue, the King James Bible translators for their part carried through with that project of common access as the justification for Anglicanism, saying the Apostle intended to include all languages and to except none.

Sacred Scripture and the Common Idiom

Translation of the Bible was undertaken in the earliest centuries because no one had the idea that the sacredness of the Bible was to be sought in its incomprehensibility. That was why Latin, Syriac, Coptic, and Gothic translations flourished. Both Athanasius and Chrysostom called for the right of the laity to be able to read the scripture. Chrysostom denied that reading the Bible was only for the clergy and monks, while Athanasius reproached heretics for barring ordinary folk from reading the scriptures. It was only the disinterest of the laity that led to scripture being withdrawn from general use. It resulted in the irony that the habit of lay disinterest was replaced by the habit of clerical monopoly that the lay people caused by their neglect! Ad hoc practice hardened into a doctrinaire rule. In defense of common access to scripture, Milton said it was fitting in view of his work of translating the Vulgate that the devil should whip Jerome in a Lenten dream for reading Cicero.[13]

The gospel is not a sealed mystery, as the King James Bible translators made clear when they shifted from the general to the specific case of the task at hand. It was no defect in the ancient prophet that he was raised to public view on the strength only of being handed a sealed book that he could not read, and in that position the prophet was mere emissary of an inaccessible and remote potentate (Isaiah 29:11), "since of an hidden treasure, and of a fountain that is sealed, there is no profit."[14] From the point of view of the moral instruction of humanity, however, awareness of God's overbearing, inscrutable will was little better—or worse—than ignorance of God's word; that fault was remedied in the fullness of time when the law regulating faith and worship was not based on race and blood but on God's salvation for all people. James I himself wrote to that effect, saying that "it is one of the golden Sentences, which Christ our Sauiour vttered to his Apostles, that there is nothing so couered, that shall not be reuealed, neither so hidde, that shall not be knowen; and whatsouever they haue spoken in darknesse, should be heard in the light."[15]

Christianity's translated nature places God at the center of the universe of cultures, with the effect of all cultures becoming equal in their status as historical bearers of scripture. For the purposes of Bible translation, all languages have merit and are necessary, yet none is indispensable in its particularity. As we know from history, many cultures, including ancient Latin, were rescued from inevitable decline—if not from certain death—by the timely intervention of Christian translation and adoption.[16] Similarly, the Christian faith was time and again salvaged from decay by the same cause. St. Augustine describes eloquently that theme of recovery and renewal in his *City of God*. Converts who learn, and the agents who taught them, were thereby refreshed from a common stream. Thus were gentile tongues anointed, and, with that, the church's range.

Outcome: Language and a Common Humanity

Having made, then, both the general point that translation is not an exercise in linguistic perfection and the specific point about the rationale for their own translation, the authors of the King James Bible assured the reader that in no way did they wish to diminish the importance of past achievements or to exaggerate their own effort. On the contrary, in paying tribute to the previous translations, they recognized the failings of their own, saying they were entitled to no higher privilege than to follow in the footsteps of their predecessors by committing their work to the favor of God, and to the judgment of the reader.[17]

The question that has nipped at the heels of Bible translators is whether the act of producing so many different versions of scripture does not perpetuate divisions among Christians, create a stumbling block for ecumenical solidarity, and undermine the church's authority and its message. In its proliferating translated versions, the Bible has become religious shrapnel, causing injury to Christian unity. In the circumstances, it would be better to restrict the scriptures to those languages that are endowed with cosmopolitan advantage and allow tribal tongues to die a natural death. After all, so the argument goes, not everyone is equipped for life in the age of global responsibility, and Bible translation would serve us all by investing in that global cause rather than invoking the specter of the antagonism that once wracked Christian Europe.

Critics argue that, even on the limited ground of nation building, Bible translation threatens a major upheaval with its focus on difference rather than on unity. Since most developing countries are strapped for resources, it is beyond dispute that they cannot provide funds equally for all languages. Better to concentrate the available resources on the languages of social and economic scale than to fritter the resources on remote and marginal tongues. Common sense requires we do nothing less.

One may briefly respond to these criticisms by pointing out that the multiplicity of languages is not the cause of division and conflict, nor is the promotion of one language the guarantee of unity and harmony. Italy, for example, has many languages without that creating violent fragmentation, whereas Northern Ireland had bitter intercommunal violence in spite of a common language between the warring Catholics and Protestants. The same can be said about the 1994 genocide in Catholic Rwanda, where the fact that Hutus and Tutsis share a common language did not prevent the outbreak of violence between them. As for cosmopolitan sophistication and material advantage, Europe's attainment in those respects did not prevent Europe's devastating wars of the twentieth century, something equally true, say, of Japan and its involvement in war. Material advancement by itself is insufficient to guarantee moral progress.

With respect to nation building, Somalia's monolingual status, including its adherence to one religion with its untranslated scripture, has not saved it from chronic wars and strife. Indeed, Somalia has become a byword for a failed state. The view that if we had one language in common we would overcome division and misunderstanding is not warranted by historical evidence and theological realism, nor is there much credibility for the idea that multiple language use impedes understanding and tolerance. Accordingly, the logic of Bible translation is unaffected by arguments concerned with the demands of peace and harmony.

Post-Western Christianity is for the most part the religion of multiple language users, in contrast to the post-Christian West where single language users, it happens, tend to predominate. By adopting languages already in use, Christianity makes local comprehension a validation of its mission. The myriad languages of the religion demonstrate the universal scope of God's mission: no one is excluded on account of scale, status, or geography. The gospel is not marooned in Bethlehem because spiritually Jesus is born in the heart of believers, wherever or whoever they are. Christian translation is about the adoption of multiple idioms and cultural domains, not about preserving an original tongue or place. The statement of Kepler (d.1630), cited above, that "the Bible speaks the language of everyman" is an affirmation about the salvific merit of "everyman's language." God speaks our language, and approves it for scripture, worship, and prayer.

The correlation between indigenous cultural revitalization and faith identity is a consistent one in the development of Christianity, beginning with the gentile transformation in the primitive church. The vernacular Bible ended the isolation of tribe and tongue, reversed or slowed the process of neglect and decline, and forged a sense of spiritual kinship. Just as the English of King Alfred was more complicated than modern English, so were vernacular languages before Bible translation. Accordingly, the simplicity of translation triggered religious currents that fostered comparative inquiry and exchange.

In a critical study of the life of Robert Moffat, the outstanding missionary linguist of southern Africa, the observation was made that the vernacular Bible bridged the old and new. It was a living book in the sense that it acquired fresh impetus in homebred tones and accents. It was impossible to ignore it. Lifting a vernacular New Testament in his hand, an African convert testified that he and his people once imagined the Bible to be a charm of the white people designed to keep off sickness and to be a trap to catch the people. He knew differently now. "We have never heard of such a thing . . . but now we not only hear with our ears, we see with our eyes, we read it, our children read it. . . . We thought it was a thing to be spoken to, but now we know it has a tongue. It speaks and will speak to the whole world."[18] Christian vernacular has the accent of a universal message, well expressed in the words of Walt Whitman in his *Song of the Open Road*: "I find letters from God dropt in the street, and every one is sign'd by God's name." In spite of linguistic and cultural difference, the capacity of human language to bear the truth of God binds us in the religious life. Being the gifts of God, all tongues and cultures serve a common purpose, so that the parts of our individual idioms share in the sum of united witness and discernment.

A translated Christianity connects with the incarnate God who in Jesus "dwelt among us . . . full of grace and truth" (John 1:14). Translation does not end our brokenness; it simply opens our eyes to a new and different reality. The fact that in the early modern period translators paid the ultimate sacrifice by laying down their lives seems a poignant testament to the mystery of the atonement of the one who is the incarnate word of God. Translation of scripture was fraught with perils and shadowed by the cross. The whole enterprise of translation seemed like fitting testimony to the God who knew the way of Calvary, and an instructive metaphor of the incarnation. Temporal setbacks evoke the deeper divine sacrifice. If there is a better way to explain the unstinting investment of consecrated labor in the cause I, for one, do not know it.

Changing Course in the Twenty-First Century

Bible translation into the vernacular confronts us with a key question not only about the mission and vocation of the church—why and to what end is the church in the world? What tasks define the marks of its true vocation?—but also what form and shape will the hopes and yearnings of the present generation take? What are the reigning vernacular idioms that translation must engage for the work of God? The church may speak eloquently and rightly of "God's work in history leaving global footprints" in the shape of new communities of faith, which in themselves, incidentally, may be adversely affected by the forces of globalization. We must, however, dig deeper: where and how are these new faith communities coming into being? What circumstances best describe their rise? What are the hopes and dreams that move them? What can we learn about the meaning of history by the growing evidence of God's work in the new church communities on the margins of power and privilege? What is the meaning of contemporary history for the church-in-mission in terms of waning old heartlands and emerging new strongholds beyond the West?

Conclusion: Old Contexts, New Horizons

In the centuries since Tyndale and Kepler, Bible translation has revealed in dramatic fashion linguistic difference and diversity as hallmarks of the Christian movement. More people worship, pray, and sing hymns in more languages in Christianity than in any other religion. By playing a necessary and indispensable role as carriers of the Christian scriptures, non-Western languages became channels of faith and understanding. In their complex variety, languages provided the indispensable channel and evidence of God's salvific promise. God *communicated* with the peoples of the world, and translation is testament of that.

The rapid, unprecedented expansion of Christianity from the second half of the twentieth century has thrown into high relief the impact of Bible translation on societies beyond the West. The suddenness and scope of the expansion,

however, have likely concealed an important theological lesson. Standard theological models of Christianity have presented it as a closed-circuit religion
whose main pathways of communication and authority have been laid in the
trusted channels of the Western canon.

Faced with this imposing system, the task of the theologian consisted in
codifying the religion, putting down stakes for its boundary, defining its form
and function, predicting and prescribing for changes, holding out against foreign matter entering it, sifting outlandish ideas, fixing the accepted qualities of
the religion, and generalizing about how God works in the world. In this view,
translation spawns syncretism, sects, heresy, and apostasy, which are to religion
what aberration, mutation, infection, and suicide are to an immutable organism. In its elegance, the system of theology reflects the neurological design of a
living organism: theology has a built-in resonance with the religion's ingrained
circuitry. This organic model of Christianity has arguably been the most influential so far, and dominates much of the academy and the printed page. Few
scholars have questioned the central assumption that the science of Christianity
has a logical universal consistency about it, yet that approach takes the poetry
out of religion.

At any rate, the pace and scale of Bible translation is witness to a far different
reality, being evidence that Christianity's neurological center has been in flux,
that its vocabulary has been growing and changing, that historical experience
has been a cumulative force, that the allotment of "neurons" has continued
because "neurogenesis" is a living process rather than a relic of evolution, that
foreign idioms have lodged in the system like oxygen in the bloodstream, and
that "localizationism" in the frontal lobe of Northern Christianity has shifted
to the central cortex of Southern Christianity where new, expanded tasks have
stimulated tolerance and diversity in the religion. Translation has shifted the
"genetic determinism" of the preserved canon by encrypting the religion with
the most diverse cultural chromosomes of other societies. Old school theology
appears like a relic in the new milieu, which may explain its reported decline in
its once hallowed cultural strongholds.

With dazzling confidence, the old theology perfected the method of etymo-
logical diagnosis and exegetical prescription without much regard to God as
living reality. Expertise in the subject required only logical rigor, not lively
accountability to revealed truth. By contrast, as Tyndale immortalized it, translation is committed to the local idiom as the crucible of faith, with new idioms

considered not as stray dialects, and to the fact that God's intervention in the Word made flesh is ground for embracing all flesh—and the words for it—as clean. The translated scripture is the charter of lived Christian experience, and the church's dynamic pathway. Bible translation is intelligent design for the dilemma of a common humanity: Given the fractures of our existential situation, how can our idioms reconcile us unless we encounter God in them? Theological science cannot discount our idioms as mere accident. In a speech on the occasion of the bicentenary of the British and Foreign Bible Society in 2004, Archbishop Rowan Williams summed up the implications of Bible translation for the church. "If scripture can be 're-created' in different languages," he wrote, "the humanity of the saviour who speaks in scripture must be an extraordinary humanity, a unique humanity. . . . Every language and culture has in it a sort of 'homing instinct' for God—deeply buried by the sin and corruption that affects all cultures, yet still there, a sleeping beauty to be revived by the word of Christ."[19]

Appendix: Statistical Summary[20]

A summary, by geographical area and type of publication, of the number of different languages and dialects in which publication of at least one book of the Bible had been registered as of December 31, 2006:

Continent or Region	Portions	Testaments	Bibles	Bibles + DC[1]	Total
Africa	218	322	163	(29)	703
Asia-Pacific	363	495	171	(37)	1,029
Europe-Middle East	112	39	61	(47)	212
Americas	153	312	42	(10)	507
Constructed Languages	2	0	1	(0)	3
Total	848	1,168	438	(123)	2,454

[1] This column is a subsection of the Bibles column. For example, there is a translation of the Deutero-canon for 47 of the 61 languages of Europe-Middle East in which the Bible has been translated.

Notes

1. Erroll F. Rhodes and Liana Lupas, eds., *The Translators to the Reader: The Original Preface of the King James Version of 1611 Revisited* (New York: American Bible Society, 1997), 34.

2. Sir Isaac Newton (1642–1727), in a work titled *The Philosophical Origins of Gentile Theology*, argued that the Bible existed in a language of perfect and exact signification—an orderly universe of meaning that could be discovered by the rule of mystical interpretation like the *abjad* method in Arabic. "The Rule I have followed has been to compare the several mystical places of scripture where the same prophetic phrase or type is used, and to fix such a signification to that phrase as agrees best with all the [other] places . . . and when I have found the necessary significations, to reject all others as the offspring of luxuriant fancy, for no more significations are to be admitted for true ones than can be proved." Only by that procedure might one gain a true and unvarying understanding of the Bible and remedy the corruptions that have crept into religion. Thus did Newton set out to remedy the problem of Christianity as a translated, and therefore as a prone-to-be-misunderstood religion. The language of scripture, Newton maintained, was unlike the languages of the world in its capacity to defy difference and historical contingency, for only such a universal and unifying language was worthy of the one universal God who spoke it (H. McLachlan, ed., *Theological Manuscripts* [Liverpool: Liverpool University Press, 1950], 119ff). See also Holquist's incisive examination of the role of language in religion and nationalism, which leads to what he calls the problem of the contradiction between the moral subject and the psychological personality, between reason and freedom, in the Enlightenment concept of the self. The Kantian subject, Holquist says, is fundamentally at odds with itself by virtue of the doomed arithmetic that requires a divided soul to be one. Bible translation offers a different contrast by taking that dilemma in a positive direction and making the word of the transcendent God transmissible in living historical idioms. The universal and particular in Bible translation transcended what Holquist indicates as the contradiction between reason and freedom, or between general truth and unique action (Michael Holquist, "Local Universes: Myths of a National Language," in Ullabeth Sätterlund Larsson, ed., *Socio-Cultural Theory and Methods: An Anthology* [Udevalla, Sweden: University of Trollhättan, *Skriftserie*, no. 6, 2001], 66–68). Something of that transcendent confidence is expressed by the translators of the King James Bible, namely, that the one God of scripture is available to us in the many forms of human communication. Accordingly, they affirmed: "Translation it is that openeth the window, to let in the light . . . that removeth the cover of the well, that we may come by the water" (Rhodes and Lupas, eds., *Translators*, 34). In the final analysis, translation of scripture is the God-given channel by which human beings by choice may rise to the status of children of God. Kepler alluded to a similar rule when he declared: "The Bible speaks the language of everyman" (cited in F. E. Manuel, *The Religion of Isaac Newton* [Oxford: Oxford University Press, 1974], 36).

3. The end and reward of scripture, the translators said, was, among other things, "repentance from dead works, newness of life, holiness, peace, joy in the Holy Ghost, fellowship with the saints" (Rhodes and Lupas, eds., *Translators*, 54).

4. Alister McGrath, *In the Beginning: the Story of the King James Bible and How It Changed a Nation, a Language, and a Culture* (Random House: New York, 2001), 67, 78–79.

5. Donald Coggan, *The English Bible* (London: Longmans, Green & Co. for the British Council and the National Book League, 1963), 19.

6. Lamin Sanneh, *Translating the Message: The Missionary Impact on Culture*, 2d edition (Maryknoll: Orbis Books, 2009), 74–76. Tyndale paid with his life for his pains. Escaping to the continent, he was betrayed by a friend and captured near Brussels in 1536. Locked up in a damp, cold dungeon on the orders of Emperor Charles V, he pleaded for items of clothing to stave off the extreme cold, and for a lamp to relieve the icy gloom. Above all, he asked for his Hebrew Bible, Hebrew grammar, and Hebrew dictionary "that I may spend my time with that study." Tyndale was tied to the stake and strangled by the hangman and then "with fire consumed." His ashes were thrown into the river to obliterate all trace of the man. Yet Tyndale's effect on the evolution of English prose and letters was immense. Long after he was gone and several generations had passed, "Tyndale's rhythms had begun to vibrate in the minds of a younger generation, and when at last the final version of the English Bible appeared . . . the spirit of Tyndale still moved through its majestic cadences . . . that mighty thing, the power of prose, was at work. . . . The book existed, though the man was dead" (Hilaire Belloc, *Cranmer, Archbishop of Canterbury, 1533–1556* [Philadelphia: J.P. Lippincott and Co., 1931], 193–94). Belloc, otherwise hostile to Tyndale, takes large liberties with his historical facts, though his judgment about Tyndale reflects the general consensus. Ironically, Tyndale's translation was surreptitiously circulated by the prior of an English Augustinian monastery whence it fell into the hands of Miles Coverdale, an Augustinian friar. Coverdale's translation, "best viewed as a compilation of other people's translations," (McGrath, *In the Beginning*, 90) was approved by the king even though Coverdale made explicit and extensive use of Tyndale (Olga S. Opfell, *The King James Bible Translators* [McFarland: Jefferson, NC and London, 1982], 17, 20). Thomas Cranmer also lost his life in the cause, being burned at the stake in 1556 on the orders of Mary Tudor. Executed with Cranmer was John Rogers, a Tyndale protégé and author of the Matthew Bible. Rogers's execution was made famous by the encouragement and comfort at the site of the execution afforded him by his wife, Adriana, and the presence of their eleven children, the youngest a suckling infant. See Foxe's *Acts and Monuments of These Latter and Perilous Days* (Book of Martyrs), 1573.

7. See John Michael Wallace-Hadrill, *The Frankish Church* (Oxford: Clarendon Press, 1983), 386.

8. Diedrich Westermann, "The Place and Function of the Vernacular in African Education," *International Review of Mission* (January 1925): 26–27.

9. Cited in Edwin W. Smith, *The Shrine of a People's Soul* (London: Livingstone, 1929), 198–99.

10. Rhodes and Lupas, eds., *Translators*, 62.

11. The translators noted that the Roman Catholic Church had never denied the translatability of Christianity and was not in principle opposed to Bible translation: the church only required a written license for it. It was that issue that drew the objections of the translators: the Catholic Church, they felt, ought to play to the script and not interpose artificial barriers between scripture and its natural milieu of translation. With the gold of scripture, Christians must not be afraid to come to the touchstone of vernacular validation. In point of fact, Catholics are best fitted to translate the Bible into English. "They have learning, and they know when a thing is well, they can *manum de tabula* ("hands off the tablet," quoting Cicero)" (Rhodes and Lupas, eds., *Translators*, 44).

12. William Tyndale, *The Obedience of a Christian Man* (London: Penguin Books, 2000), 24. Tyndale thrust himself into the political limelight by his determination to wrest religion

from political sponsorship, and the clergy from being minions of the state. Religious corruption and political tyranny had for Tyndale a common source in the gelding of the church. As such, Tyndale was a precursor of modern politics.

13. Milton, Aeropagitica, *Complete Poetry and Selected Prose* (New York: The Modern Library, 1950), 688.

14. Rhodes and Lupas, eds, *Translators*, 45.

15. Cited in Adam Nicolson, *God's Secretaries: The Making of the King James Bible* (New York: Harper Collins, 2003), 144.

16. W. H. C. Frend, *The Rise of Christianity* (Philadelphia: Fortress Press, 1984), 560.

17. The translators testified: "We are like dwarves sitting on the shoulders of giants. We see more, and things that are more distant, than they did, not because our sight is superior or because we are taller than they, but because they raise us up, and by their great stature add to ours" (cited in McGrath, *In the Beginning*, 176).

18. Smith, *Shrine*, 190.

19. Archbishop Rowan Williams, "Sermon at the Service to celebrate the Bicentenary of the British and Foreign Bible Society," pp. 1–2, St. Paul's Cathedral, London, March 8, 2004 (www.archbishopofcanterbury.org/1171).

20. The information here is taken from the United Bible Societies *Scripture Language Report 2007*, accessed at www.drustvo-svds.si/kdo_smo/SLR2007.pdf, November 4, 2010. An updated list of Bible translations can be found in Sanneh, *Translating the Message*.

2.3 The Body of Christ

1 Corinthians 11:23-27 and 12:12-13, 27

DANIEL A. MADIGAN

1 Corinthians 11:23–27

²³For I received from the Lord what I also handed on to you, that the Lord Jesus on the night when he was betrayed took a loaf of bread, ²⁴and when he had given thanks, he broke it and said, "This is my body that is for you. Do this in remembrance of me." ²⁵In the same way he took the cup also, after supper, saying, "This cup is the new covenant in my blood. Do this, as often as you drink it, in remembrance of me." ²⁶For as often as you eat this bread and drink the cup, you proclaim the Lord's death until he comes.

²⁷Whoever, therefore, eats the bread or drinks the cup of the Lord in an unworthy manner will be answerable for the body and blood of the Lord.

1 Corinthians 12:12–13, 27

¹²For just as the body is one and has many members, and all the members of the body, though many, are one body, so it is with Christ. ¹³For in the one Spirit we were all baptized into one body—Jews or Greeks, slaves or free—and we were all made to drink of one Spirit.
²⁷Now you are the body of Christ and individually members of it.

The two passages to be considered here have, on the face of it, very little to do with translation or with scripture. So why were they chosen? In my previous chapter in this volume, I argue that in the Christian understanding the Word of God is expressed not in the first place in scripture, but in the Incarnation, in the "body language" of Jesus Christ. What follows from this is that the sacred language of Christianity is not the Aramaic of Jesus, nor the Greek of the New Testament, but the same body language in which, as John's Gospel puts it, God expressed the Word in our world.

Therefore, the two passages discussed here, both from Paul's first letter to the Christians in the city of Corinth, have been chosen because both speak about the body. We are not speaking here about the translation of scripture, because at the point Paul is writing there is no particularly Christian scripture. When Paul and other Christians at the time spoke of scripture, they meant the Hebrew scriptures, since they basically saw themselves as a community within Judaism. This letter we are examining will eventually come to be considered scripture, and will eventually be translated in various ways, but for the moment we are focusing on the question of the body.

I want to discuss first the passage from chapter 12 of 1 Corinthians. From what we can make out, the Corinthian community to which Paul was writing had various kinds of divisions and factions in it. In verses 4–11, Paul refers to the diversity of roles in the community, and then in verses 12–13 he uses the image of the body to explain how this diversity is nonetheless in reality an organic unity. Paul then continues in verses 14–26 to speak about the organic nature of the body and the way the parts fit and work together, how they affect one another and protect one another, before declaring in verse 27: "Now you are the body of Christ and individually members of it."

If this is the case—if the Christian community is to be understood as Christ's body, and if Christ is God's Word spoken in the flesh—then it follows that the Christian community, when it is true to itself, is a kind of ongoing incarnation. It has the mission (in the sense of the Arabic *risāla*) of expressing that same Word in an embodied way—not merely by what it says, for talk is cheap—but by how it lives out the love of God that was embodied in Jesus Christ: in loving, in humble service, in healing, feeding, liberating, and reconciling.

This is a tall order, and one in which Christians so often fail. Yet it needs to be underlined that this is a communal mission. In Paul's mind it is not simply the effort of the individual Christian that counts; he does not imagine that each believer is the body of Christ. Indeed, such individualism is the very problem he is confronting in the church of Corinth. It is as an organic unity that we express the Word. The ongoing process of translation—that is, the process of making the Word present and understood across various cultures and in various situations—is an act that we do with our embodiedness as a community.

We can relate this to the passage from John 16 considered earlier in this volume. I do not want to suggest that Paul thinks in exactly the same terms as John, but I believe the two can shed light on one another. In John 16:13, Jesus says, "When the Spirit of truth comes, he will guide you into all the truth." For Paul it is God's Spirit that is animating the body in its diverse parts. God's Spirit is using the whole of this body-community to do what Jesus spoke about: to continue the work of expressing God's truth. In expressing that truth in the flesh, by its loving as Jesus loved, the community comes to an ever deeper understanding of the truth—not merely an intellectual understanding, but one that is felt in one's very body. The Spirit-animated community not only understands the truth more deeply, but also expresses it more clearly.

One aspect of the community's embodiedness—one might even say it is the *core* of that embodiedness—brings us to the other of the two passages, 1 Corinthians 11:23–27, which is about what Christians call the Eucharist, from *"eucharistēsas"* ("having given thanks") in verse 24. This is the earliest written account we have of the words and actions of Jesus at the supper "on the night that he was betrayed," since Paul is writing his letter before the Gospels were written. The Christians, we know from the Acts of the Apostles (2:42, 46), met from the very beginning to celebrate the Breaking of the Bread, the Eucharist, which was a specifically Christian act. Even so, as long as the Temple in Jerusalem was standing, they still continued to pray there with their fellow Jews. They met in their homes for the Breaking of the Bread, which was the re-presenting— the making present once more—of Jesus's Last Supper, the supper that is, perhaps, referred to in *Surat al-Mā'ida* (Qur'ān 5:112–15).

Again the context is the problem of disunity in this community at Corinth. Paul has heard from various reports that when the Christians of Corinth meet for this ritual meal, they are betraying it in some sense by their disunity (1 Corinthians 11:17–22). Such fellowship meals were a common practice in Hellenistic culture and the Christians' meeting for the Lord's Supper, as Paul calls it here, seems to have been grafted onto that familiar custom. Corinth was a very large city in which the Christian community included the well-to-do as well as the poor. What Paul seems to have understood from the reports is that the rich turned up early because they were people of leisure, they had plenty of time to come for the common meal, and they could eat and drink as much as they liked. The poor, who had to come from their work, struggled to get there, and then when they arrived were treated as the poor are treated in most places where the rich are eating and drinking. Though this kind of inequality at the fellowship meal is a common theme among ancient writers, to Paul it is a betrayal of the nature of the Church; it is a betrayal of this ongoing work of being the Body of Christ and therefore of expressing the Word. What the Corinthians are doing, he tells them, is not the Eucharist—it is not "the Lord's Supper" (*kyriakon deipnon* v. 20) but rather each one's individual supper (*idion deipnon* v. 21). Then, in verses 23–27, Paul describes the actions and words of Jesus with which the Lord's Supper is instituted.[1]

Paul is outraged—I think the word is not too strong—about what is going on at these gatherings of the Christians in Corinth, at what should be the action of reliving the Last Supper. What the Corinthians are doing is unworthy, since they are eating "without recognizing the body" (v. 29). Paul tells them that they are falsely pretending to be the body of Christ by behaving in this way: they are still looking down on the poor, and still thinking first of themselves and their pride of social place. So they are betraying the body of Christ and are answerable for it (v. 27).

The Eucharist is so central to the self-understanding of Christians that there is no end to what could be said about this passage. However, I would like to suggest for reflection a theme that has resonances in all three of the Abrahamic traditions. Paul uses the term remembrance (*anamnēsis*) twice here. This same word is used in the Greek version of the Hebrew scriptures to translate *zikkār-ōn*—from the Hebrew verb *zākar*, which, of course, is cognate with the Arabic *dhakira*. Muslims will recognize the importance of the idea and action of *dhikr*: the Qur'ān as *dhikr*, as a reminder; the importance of *dhikr* in Muslim spirituality, recalling the names of God. In all three traditions, this is not just remembering as we memorize our multiplication tables or verb paradigms. This *anamnēsis/zikkārōn/dhikr* is somehow a making-present of, and a participation in, the great past actions of God in saving and revealing. Remembering is in some sense re-living.[2] In remembering the names of God, we are immersing ourselves in those attributes of God—life, mercy, knowledge, truth, compassion, love, forgiveness—and so seek to become more merciful, truthful, compassionate, and so on.

For Christians, too, this *anamnēsis*, remembering what Jesus did by doing it again, is essential to being the body of Christ. For most of the Christian tradition, it is in the celebration of the Eucharist that we become most fully the body of Christ—which explains Paul's outrage at what is happening in Corinth. For Christians this is a remembrance in a double sense, because it is likely that the Last Supper was a Passover meal, the meal in which the Jewish community remembers, in that active sense of which we have been speaking, the great act of God in freeing his people from the slavery of Egypt. So this passage prompts us to explore this common notion of *dhikr*: the remembrance, the making real once more by recalling. This is the major task before us as believers in a Word of God spoken historically in our world: how to make it real in the present so that it continues to speak to the world.

Notes

1. Paul's expression at the beginning of verse 23 ("For I received from the Lord what I also passed on to you") is somewhat like the introduction to a ḥadīth. He is saying that these are the actual words that he has heard and is passing on. This is also the style of rabbinic tradition.

2. The English word gives us an opportunity to play with Paul's notion of the body's various members—though this has nothing to do with the real etymology of the word. Remembering is a kind of re-embodying.

2.4 An Arabic Qur'ān
Qur'ān 12:1–2; 14:4; 16:103; 26:192–99; 46:12

MUHAMMAD ABDEL HALEEM

12:1–2

¹*Alif Lam Ra*
These are the verses of the Scripture that makes things clear—²We have sent it down as an Arabic Qur'an so that you [people] may understand.

14:4

We have never sent a messenger who did not use his own people's language to make things clear for them. But still God leaves whoever He will to stray, and guides whoever He will: He is the Almighty, the All Wise.

16:103

We know very well that they say, "It is a man who teaches him," but the language of the person they allude to is foreign, while this revelation is in clear Arabic.

26:192–99

¹⁹²Truly, this Qur'an has been sent down by the Lord of the Worlds: ¹⁹³the Trustworthy Spirit brought it down ¹⁹⁴to your heart [Prophet], so that you could bring warning ¹⁹⁵in a clear Arabic tongue. ¹⁹⁶This was foretold in the scriptures of earlier religions. ¹⁹⁷Is it not proof enough for them that the learned men of the Children of Israel have recognized it? ¹⁹⁸If We had sent it down to someone who was not an Arab, ¹⁹⁹and he had recited it to them, they still would not have believed in it.

[In verse 193, the "Trustworthy Spirit" is generally understood to mean the Angel Gabriel.]

46:12

Yet the scripture of Moses was revealed before it as a guide and a mercy, and this is a scripture confirming it in the Arabic language to warn those who do evil and bring good news for those who do good.

The passages to be considered here have been selected because of their relevance to the theme that the revelation given by God in the Qur'ān is in Arabic. Here I will briefly mention some key points from these passages, some of which have already been discussed in the chapter titled "Translating the Qur'ān," in this volume.

All of these passages are of Meccan origin and reflect the encounter between the Prophet and the Meccan disbelievers, who rejected the message of the Qur'ān and, indeed, the very possibility that Muhammad, an Arab from among themselves, could be the bearer of a divine revelation. The general purpose of these and also of many other similar Meccan passages is, therefore, to answer the incredulity of the Meccan Arabs toward the idea that an Arab could receive a revelation. Unlike the Jews or Christians, who were used to revelations coming to them and to individual human beings, the Arabs could not believe that a mere mortal could receive revelation. Some asserted, "God has sent nothing down to a mere mortal" (6:91); they also asked: "What sort of messenger is this? He eats food and walks about in the marketplaces. Why has no angel been sent down to help him with his warnings?" (25:7). The Qur'ān had to point out that all previous messengers were men who ate food (21:7–8). In response to the Meccans' denial of the possibility of prophethood being bestowed upon mere mortals, the Qur'ān asks, "Who was it who sent down the Scripture, which Moses brought as a light and a guide to people?" (6:91). The crucial point in this context is that the Qur'ān also explains that every previous messenger had received his revelation in the language of the people to be addressed, so that the divine communication would be clear. In the words of one of the passages selected above: "We have never sent a messenger who did not use his own people's language to make things clear for them" (14:4). Another of the selected passages makes the same point: in response to the accusation that the Qur'ān is untrue (46:11), it asserts that "the scripture of Moses was revealed before it [the Qur'ān] as a guide and a mercy, and this is a scripture confirming it in the Arabic language to warn those who do evil and bring good news for those who do good" (46:12).

Thus a major emphasis of these passages is that the Qur'ān was revealed in Arabic in order to ensure clear communication. The word *mubīn* ("clear") occurs three times, once applied to the Qur'ān itself (12:2) and twice to the Arabic in which it is revealed (16:103; 26:195); in another passage (14:4) it is said that every messenger spoke in the language of his people *liyubayyina lahum* ("to make things clear for them"), where the verb *bayyana* is cognate with *mubīn*. This great stress on clarity is linked to the fundamental purpose of revelation, namely that people should understand and therefore have no excuse for not believing. In this context the Qur'ān repeatedly employs the conjunction of purpose *la'allakum / la'allahum* ("so that you/they may . . ."), as at 12:2: "We have sent it down as an Arabic Qur'ān so that you [people] may understand" (see also 20:163; 39:28; 41:3; 43:3).

One of the selected passages (16:103) refers to the fact that the Qur'ān is in Arabic in response to a specific charge against the Prophet. Here the disbelievers are reported as asserting: "It is a man who teaches him [Muhammad]." In other words, it is alleged by the disbelievers that what is being claimed as divine revelation has in fact come to Muhammad through ordinary human channels. Commentators identify the man in question as one or another foreign individual in Mecca, with some suggesting a Christian blacksmith. The succinct retort made by the Qur'ān is that the language of the man they allude to is "foreign" (*a'jamī*), while the Qur'ānic revelation is in "clear Arabic." In Arabic dictionaries *a'jam* and *a'jamī* have the meaning of "mute" (*akhras*). In another derivation *ista'jam* means "became silent." It is stated that *a'jamī* means not just foreign but also lacking the ability to express oneself.[1] The argument produced in the Qur'ān must have related to an individual who could not express himself and therefore could not have produced the language of the Qur'ān, which is very clear Arabic—*'arabiyun mubīn*. There is no record that anyone refuted this simple but effective argument.

The emphasis in the passages considered here on the fact that the Qur'ān was revealed in Arabic has been misinterpreted in two ways that should be briefly mentioned. First, it has long been claimed by some non-Muslims that the mission of Muhammad was, on the evidence of the Qur'ān itself, only for the Arabs. However, the Qur'ān insists that it comes to all people (*kāffatan li al-nās*): "It is to all people that We have sent you [Prophet] to bring good news and warning" (34:28). Second, the passages considered here do not justify the view, held by some Muslims in the classical period, that the Qur'ān should not be translated. On this point I refer the reader to the fuller discussion in chapter 2.1 of this volume.

However, although it is both permissible and desirable for the Qur'ān to be translated into other languages, in another sense this is, of course, an impossible task. The divine origin of the Qur'ān, and the fact that it is in Arabic, mean that for Muslims the Arabic Qur'ān is the very word of God. This makes it difficult for them to think of it being translated into any other language while remaining the word of God. Together with this fundamental religious point there are also literary factors to take into consideration. The very complex language and style of the Qur'ān, concise as it is, its rich vocabulary and structure that show multiplicity of meanings, and the surpassing sound-effect that enhances meaning and gives the Qur'ān a grandeur in Arabic that is difficult to achieve in any approximation—all these factors have contributed to the belief that the Qur'ān is untranslatable. Muslim and non-Muslim translators have confirmed this. Translators who really understand the complexity and effect of the Arabic Qur'ān, after doing all they can with the translation, still feel that there is a massive loss of meaning and effect. If this applies to all great masterpieces of literature, it certainly applies all the more to the Qur'ān. Any translation is no more than a pale shadow of the original and does not have the effect described by the Qur'ān itself: "God has sent down the most beautiful of all teachings: a Scripture that is consistent and draws comparisons; that causes the skins of those in awe of their Lord to quiver. Then their skins and their hearts soften at the mention of God: such is God's guidance" (39:23).

Note

1. *Al-Mu'jama al-wasīṭ* (Cairo: Arabic Language Academy, n.d.), under the entry '-j-m.

2.5 The Divine and Human Origins of the Bible
Exodus 32:15–16; Jeremiah 1:9; 2 Timothy 3:16–17; Luke 1:1–4; 1 Corinthians 7:10–13; Mark 5:41

JOHN AZUMAH

Exodus 32:15–16

[15] Then Moses turned and went down from the mountain, carrying the two tablets of the covenant in his hands, tablets that were written on both sides, written on the front and on the back. [16]The tablets were the work of God, and the writing was the writing of God, engraved upon the tablets.

Jeremiah 1:9

Then the Lord put out his hand and touched my mouth; and the Lord said to me, "Now I have put my words in your mouth."

2 Timothy 3:16–17

[16]All scripture is inspired by God and is useful for teaching, for reproof, for correction, and for training in righteousness, [17]so that everyone who belongs to God may be proficient, equipped for every good work.

Luke 1:1–4

[1]Since many have undertaken to set down an orderly account of the events that have been fulfilled among us, [2]just as they were handed on to us by those who from the beginning were eyewitnesses and servants of the word, [3]I too decided, after investigating everything carefully from the very first, to write an orderly account for you, most excellent Theophilus, [4]so that you may know the truth concerning the things about which you have been instructed.

1 Corinthians 7:10–13

[10]To the married I give this command—not I but the Lord—that the wife should not separate from her husband [11](but if she does separate, let her remain unmarried or else be reconciled to her husband), and that the husband should not divorce his wife. [12]To the rest

92

I say—I and not the Lord—that if any believer has a wife who is an unbeliever, and she consents to live with him, he should not divorce her. ¹³And if any woman has a husband who is an unbeliever, and he consents to live with her, she should not divorce him.

Mark 5:41

He took her by the hand and said to her, "*Talitha cum,*" which means, "Little girl, get up!"

M y aim is not to give a detailed commentary on each of the selected biblical passages, but rather, with some reference to these texts, to explore the underlying theme of the divine and human origins of the Bible. Like many other Christian theological students, in my early stages at seminary I had the experience of having my understanding of the Bible as God's word challenged and reshaped by the questions raised by my professors. A previously unexamined notion of the Bible as having somehow descended from heaven in its present form was exposed to questions about the diversity of its contents and the human reality of its origins, its contexts, and the processes of its composition. The underlying question was how to understand the Bible as having both human and divine origins.

This dual reality is suggested by the range of biblical texts I have chosen. At one end of the spectrum, one passage speaks of God writing his word on the tablets given to Moses (Exodus 32:16). Here the understanding seems to be of an exclusively divine act of communication. God's servant may have a role in faithfully passing on God's word but it has come into being in a way that is quite external to him. A different model appears in the prophet Jeremiah's account of his call: "Then the Lord put out his hand and touched my mouth; and the Lord said to me, 'Now I have put my words in your mouth'" (Jeremiah 1:9). Again, the initiative is entirely God's, but the placing of the words in the prophet's mouth suggests a greater degree of human involvement; the prophet will at least have to give utterance to the word, even if it is not ultimately his own.

A different model again occurs with the reference to scripture as "inspired by God" (2 Timothy 3:16). "Inspired" (*theopneustos* = breathed by God) suggests the activity of the Holy Spirit (*pneuma*); elsewhere in the New Testament the Holy Spirit is said to have "moved" or carried along those who delivered prophecies (2 Peter 1:20–21). It is this concept of inspiration by the Holy Spirit that has, perhaps, become the main way in which Christians have understood the divine origins of the Bible. Biblical inspiration is seen as the work of the Holy Spirit, using the authors of the different parts of the Bible but without setting aside their personalities and faculties.

The inspiration of the biblical authors by the Holy Spirit is a concept that allows for the divine and the human working together. It is also a model that has been understood in various ways, often reflecting wider understandings of what is at work in the processes of human thought and creativity. The concept of inspiration can thus be seen as a kind of divinely guided process of human intuition, with the writers of scripture intuitively gaining insight into God's truth. Or again inspiration can be seen in terms of God illuminating or influencing the writers' minds.

What is common to all such understandings of inspiration, however, is recognition, to varying degrees, of the human element in scripture. Even if scripture is seen as ultimately the word of God, the writers of scripture are seen as actively engaged in its production. An interesting illustration of this point is that New Testament references to Old Testament texts frequently attribute the words to their human authors; Moses, David, and Isaiah, for example, are referred to in a short section of Paul's letter to the Romans (10:19–20, 11:9). In the context of Christian-Muslim dialogue, it is illuminating to note that the readiness we find in the New Testament to introduce a quotation from scripture with, for example, the words "Isaiah is so bold as to say" (Romans 10:20) is not paralleled in Islamic discourse. Muslims always attribute the words of the Qur'ān to God, never to Muhammad.

Christian reflection on what is meant by the divine inspiration of the scriptures also needs to take into consideration what these scriptures themselves say about the engagement of their authors in their composition. In another of the selected passages (Luke 1:1–4), for example, Luke speaks openly of the efforts he has made in his work on his gospel. He speaks of "investigating everything carefully" and writing "an orderly account." This is, in one sense, an ordinary human writer going about composing a narrative in an ordinary way. While Christians recognize a fundamental underlying unity across the four gospels, they are therefore also able to acknowledge and explore the differences between them, arising naturally as specific human beings wrote with specific communities in mind.

Thus the distinctive formation, the personality traits, and the particular contexts of the different scriptural authors all come into play. Consider, for example, the very different temperaments reflected in the prophecies of Jeremiah and

Ezekiel. Paul is another biblical writer whose personality is vividly conveyed in some of his writings. In one of the selected passages there is an interesting example of his very self-conscious distinction between teaching that he can attribute directly to Jesus himself and guidance that he introduces with the words "I say—I and not the Lord . . ." (1 Corinthians 7:12).

The Bible is an account of God's interaction with and through the people of Israel, of God's personal and direct involvement in and through the person, life, death, and resurrection of Jesus Christ, and of God continuing to work through the Holy Spirit in the lives and deeds of the early Christians. The Bible witnesses to all of this and is therefore an account of a conversation, an interaction, an engagement between God and the creation, especially humankind. The Bible is a product of a dialogue, not a monologue. Hence it has both divine and human origins and can at the same time be called both the word of God and also the word of the human beings who were its writers.

Although, according to Psalm 119:89, the word of the Lord "is firmly fixed in heaven," the idea that the Bible has existed eternally in heaven is not a part of traditional Christian teaching. Indeed, the fact that Christians do not hold such a belief is another significant distinction between Christianity and Islam. For the Christian tradition the eternal Word of God is not a scripture but the personal expression of the mind of God. "In the beginning was the Word, and the Word was with God, and the Word was God" (John 1:1). The prologue to John's Gospel, beginning thus, leads to the affirmation that "the Word became flesh and lived among us" (1:14). The eternal Word of God is made known through the Incarnation, in the person of Jesus of Nazareth. This conviction at the heart of the Christian faith tells us that the purpose of divine revelation is not ultimately to communicate information but to give personal knowledge of God. It is natural that such revelation should work through the Incarnation; it is in the flesh and blood of Jesus, his life, death, and resurrection that the eternal and universal Word of God is made known to us.

It follows that while the words spoken by Jesus were of great importance to his disciples and then to the early Christian communities, his words were not in themselves seen as the very heart of revelation. It is again significant in the context of Christian-Muslim dialogue that there does not appear to have been an overriding concern among the early Christians to remember and record the actual words spoken by Jesus in the original Aramaic. Some fragments of the original Aramaic have indeed been preserved and an example is included as one of the selected texts (*Talitha cum*, meaning "Little girl, get up," at Mark 5:41).

However, such Aramaic fragments are the exceptions that prove the rule and it is clear that what the early Christians identified as being of the greatest significance in Jesus was not the original words and syllables spoken by him. The heart of the matter lay elsewhere, in who Jesus was, in what he had done, and in his ongoing risen presence. Here we are echoing a point made elsewhere in this volume: if one has to identify Christianity's "sacred language" this would have to be not Hebrew, Aramaic, Greek, or Latin but rather flesh-and-blood, the language in which God revealed his eternal Word.[1]

Before concluding this discussion we should also recognize the pattern of connections between the points made so far and the wider shape of Christian faith and practice. The Christian faith does not allow for mere profession of beliefs but calls us to participate in the divine life. Just as God chose not merely to send us letters but came down to us, participating in our human life, taking on our flesh and living among us, so we also are called to participate in God's life. This call to participation is seen especially in the sacraments of Baptism and Holy Communion, in which we are immersed in Christ and share in his life.

Through this participation in Christ, Christians find that they are no longer detached observers of the story told in the Bible. This story draws us in, so that it becomes our story. Equally, our own stories become part of this bigger story. Scripture is thus no longer the story just of Israel and the early church. It is not the story of a particular nation or people. Scripture becomes an African story, an Asian story, an American story. All nations under heaven are called to participate in this story and so also to contribute to it. As Christians participate and contribute to the story, they become the story itself, "a letter of Christ . . . written not with ink but with the Spirit of the living God, not on tablets of stone but on tablets of human hearts" (2 Corinthians 3:3).

I teach at an institute in Ghana where many different languages are represented. When we study a particular biblical passage together we sometimes read it in a number of different languages, maybe five, sometimes as many as ten. It is amazing how much different translations bring into and out of one passage. In discussion of one word or concept, such as "sin" for example, it is very enriching to hear the different translations and to listen to the interpretations offered by speakers of the different languages.

Again we are revisiting a theme explored in greater depth elsewhere in this volume, that of the translation of scripture.[2] Translation is so critical because it enables people to recognize and to own scripture as their own story. The story of the first Pentecost (in Acts 2), when the pouring out of the Holy Spirit enabled the disciples to declare God's word in the different languages of the people gathered in Jerusalem, is a key narrative serving as a warrant for translation into different languages.

Within the church's mission to "make disciples of all nations" (Matthew 28:19), the question of human language is thus of very great importance. The task of the church is not to strip individuals of their culture, giving them new names and new clothes, but rather to baptize them within and with their culture so that redemption touches not just them as individuals but also the cultures to which they belong. Within cultures languages are of central importance; within this redemptive process it is therefore essential that languages do not disappear but rather are taken up and used in worthy ways, above all for praising God.

I once worked in an inner city church in an area in Ghana that was infested with drugs and crime. After three years we finished our work and were leaving and the chief of the area called me and said "I want to thank you people for coming here." As he didn't go to church himself I asked what he wanted to thank us for. He said "Since the church came here, the children have stopped using the local language to sing profane music. I hear them singing Bible songs in the local language and I'm so pleased that the language is now being used in that way, instead of in obscenities and abuse and in all kinds of other unworthy ways."

That story may seem unconnected to where this chapter began. The link, however, is that to recognize the interplay of the divine and the human in the origins of the Bible is not an isolated observation but rather coheres with the central dynamic running through the Christian faith. The God whose ultimate self-revelation is through the Word-made-flesh participates in our human lives and calls us to participate in the divine life, which is also to say that our human lives are drawn into the story told by the Bible. As this happens, human cultures are transformed and more and more human languages join the chorus of praise of the God who is our Creator and Redeemer.

Notes

1. Daniel A. Madigan, "Particularity, Universality, and Finality: Insights from the Gospel of John."

2. Lamin Sanneh, "Translation and the Incarnate Word: Scripture and the Frontier of Languages."

2.6 The Self-Perception and the Originality of the Qur'ān
Qur'ān 2:23–24; 3:44; 10:15; 69:38–47

ABDULLAH SAEED

2:23–24

[23]If you have doubts about the revelation We have sent down to Our servant, then produce a single sura like it—enlist whatever supporters you have other than God—if you truly [think you can]. [24]If you cannot do this—and you never will—then beware of the Fire prepared for the disbelievers, whose fuel is men and stones.

[Verse 23, "whatever supporters": literally "whatever witnesses." Razi interprets this as referring either to their idols or to their leaders.]

3:44

This is an account of things beyond your knowledge that We reveal to you [Muhammad]: you were not present among them when they cast lots to see which of them should take charge of Mary, you were not present with them when they argued [about her].

["When they cast lots . . ." refers to the priests.]

10:15

When Our clear revelations are recited to them, those who do not expect to meet with Us say, "Bring [us] a different Qur'an, or change it." [Prophet], say, "It is not for me to change it of my own accord; I only follow what is revealed to me, for I fear the torment of an awesome Day, if I were to disobey my Lord."

69:38–47

[38]So I swear by what you can see [39]and by what you cannot see: [40]this [Qur'an] is the speech of an honoured messenger, [41]not the words of a poet—how little you believe!—[42]nor the words of a soothsayer—how little you reflect! [43]This [Qur'an] is a message sent down from the Lord of the Worlds: [44]if [the Prophet] had attributed some fabrication to Us, [45]We would certainly have seized his right hand [46]and cut off his lifeblood, [47]and none of you could have defended him.

[Verse 46, "lifeblood": literally "artery."]

98

T he divine origin of the Qur'ān is an issue that has been questioned since
God revealed his word, the Qur'ān, to the Prophet Muhammad in the
seventh century CE. During the Prophet's time, his opponents accused him of
having authored the Qur'ān through the creative power of jinn[1], calling him a
poet and a soothsayer. Many also tried to prove the human authorship of the
Qur'ān by creating their own "revealed" texts similar to the Qur'ān, but from
a Muslim point of view they failed to produce anything like the Qur'ān. Muslims believe that the Qur'ān is the essential miracle of the Prophet Muhammad
and that the revelation he communicated to his people from God cannot be
matched by anyone because it is utterly unique. No one other than God could
produce a book that matches the quality of the Qur'ān.

This chapter briefly explores the ideas of the originality and inimitability of
the Qur'ān by looking at the Qur'ān's self-perception, or how the Qur'ān sees
itself. The Qur'ān's confidence in its authenticity, accuracy, and reliability is
significant because these notions have had a strong influence and impact on
how Islamic tradition saw the Qur'ān. They also have important ramifications
for interfaith relations and how the Qur'ān—and Muslims—view, for example,
the scriptures of other religious traditions like Judaism and Christianity today.

The Qur'ān refers to itself as a glorious record, inscribed on the Preserved
Tablet in the Heavens (85:22), that was sent down from God to earth by the
angel Gabriel (26:193). It describes itself as the word of God (9:6), not that of a
human being or jinn, and argues that no one has added to its composition. The
Qur'ān also emphasizes that although it was in Arabic, the language of the
people of Mecca, its stories were unfamiliar to the Arabs and thus could not
have been composed by a human author like the Prophet. It asserts that it is a
guide for all people and that it contains great wisdom and is easy to understand.
Finally, the Qur'ān perceives itself to be immutable and unchangeable for all
times; it will remain so forever because God will protect it (15:9).

The Originality of the Revelation

The Qur'ān is clear in its statement that the Prophet did not author, compile,
or change the Qur'ān in any way. He simply did not have the authority to do
so. The Qur'ān says: "When our clear revelations are recited to them, those
who do not expect to meet with Us say, 'Bring [us] a different Qur'an, or change

it'. [Prophet], say, 'It is not for me to change it of my own accord; I only follow what is revealed to me, for I fear the torment of an awesome Day, if I were to disobey my Lord'" (10:15).

The Qur'ān states that it comes from God in its entirety, word for word. The same point is emphasized in Qur'ān 69:43–47, where it affirms that it is a message sent down from the Lord of the Worlds. It stresses that if the Prophet had fabricated even a part of the Qur'ān and attributed it to God, then God would have "seized his right hand and cut off his life-blood." The conviction that the Prophet could not have fabricated the Qur'ān and attributed it to God is a message that is continually emphasized in the Qur'ān.

To demonstrate that the Prophet Muhammad could not have authored it, the Qur'ān points to the fact that many of the "stories" narrated in the Qur'ān were unknown to the Prophet before they were revealed because the events within these stories took place long before his time. Referring to the account of Mary, Qur'ān 3:44 emphasizes: "This is an account of things beyond your knowledge that we reveal to you [Muhammad]; you were not present among them when they cast lots to see which of them should take charge of Mary, you were not present with them when they argued [about her]." As Mary lived centuries before the Prophet was born, and the stories were unfamiliar to the Arabs of Mecca, the argument is that the only way that the Prophet could have narrated this story was if God had revealed it to him. The Qur'ān states that it has the most beautiful stories (12:2–3), true stories (3:62; 18:13), which are new, previously unknown to the people of Mecca, the Prophet's opponents, and the Prophet himself. If that is the case, they must have come from God.

The Accusation That the Prophet Was a Poet, Soothsayer, and Madman

There is widespread consensus in the Islamic tradition on the question of the origins of the Qur'ān. For Muslims, God "inscribed" the Qur'ān, in a language that was known to Him, onto what is referred to as the "Preserved Tablet" in the Heavens (85:22). From there God conveyed the Qur'ān to the angel Gabriel in a language that the angel could understand and he, in turn, communicated it to the Prophet Muhammad in Arabic, the Prophet's native language. Muslims believe that the Prophet communicated the Qur'ān to his followers verbatim, in Arabic, as he received it, and that no words of the Qur'ān were changed as it was communicated from God to the Prophet Muhammad via the Angel Gabriel. This theological position is widely held in Islamic tradition, although there are some minor disagreements on the nature of the language in which the Qur'ān existed in the Heavens before its revelation to the Prophet Muhammad.

Again and again the Qur'ān emphasizes that in its entirety it has come from God, without any authorship, influence, or contribution from a human being or jinn. The Qur'ān says, "So I swear by what you can see and by what you cannot see. This [Qur'an] is the utterance of an honoured messenger [the Angel Gabriel], not the words of a poet—how little you believe!—nor the words of a soothsayer—how little you reflect!" (69:38–42). The affirmation in these verses that the Qur'ān was transmitted by an "honoured messenger" (understood to be Gabriel), and was not the words of a soothsayer or poet, addresses allegations that arose during the Prophet's time that stemmed, in part, from the Meccan Arabs' conception of poetry and similar texts. By relating the text of the Qur'ān to human prose they were familiar with, the Meccans were, in essence, challenging the divine origin of the Qur'ān.

The people of Mecca believed that the creativity of poets was closely connected to the jinn. The Meccans believed in the existence of jinn, and with the advent of Islam that belief continued. For instance, one of the chapters of the Qur'ān is named *Jinn*. According to Muslim understanding, jinn are like human beings in that they are required to worship God.

The Meccans believed that jinn were able to access heavenly knowledge because of their spiritual nature. At the time of the Prophet, many Meccans thought that jinn could possess people and convey information from heaven to them. These utterances could then be communicated to others, through blessings, curses, and other forms of speech that had relevance to society.

When the Prophet started reciting the early Qur'ānic texts, people immediately noticed that these texts had certain similarities to texts they were familiar with from the pre-Islamic period, such as oaths, prophecies, blessings, curses, and the like. They were also structured using familiar rhymed prose (referred to as *saj'* in Arabic). Thus the Meccans concluded that the Qur'ānic texts were nothing more than the kinds of texts they were familiar with in their culture. For them the Prophet was receiving the Qur'ān through his connection to jinn and they accused him of being possessed by jinn (a *majnūn,* or a madman), a poet, and soothsayer.

The Qur'ān's Challenge to Its Opponents

The Qur'ān's response to those who made such accusations is unequivocal, condemning in a number of verses those who claimed that the Prophet was the author of the Qur'ān. It also issues a challenge to those who doubt the divine origin of the revelation—to produce a Qur'ān like it, even one single sūra (chapter): "If you have doubts about the revelation We have sent down to our servant then produce a single sura like it—enlist whatever supporters you have other than God—if you truly think you can. If you cannot do this—and you never will—then beware of the Fire prepared for the disbelievers, whose fuel is men and stones" (2:23–24). This is not the only mention of the challenge: "If they say, 'He has invented it himself,' say, 'Then produce ten invented suras like it, and call in whoever you can beside God, if you are truthful.' If they do not answer you, then you will all know that it is sent down containing knowledge from God, and that there is no god but Him" (11:13–14). The Qur'ān concludes that not even the entirety of humankind together with all the jinn could produce the like of the Qur'ān: "Even if all mankind and jinn came together to produce something like this Qur'an, they could not produce anything like it, however much they helped each other" (17:88).

For Muslims, this challenge remains and, from their point of view, as no one has ever produced the like of the Qur'ān, its divine origin cannot be doubted. However, some have attempted to take up the challenge. Islamic history and literature record that before the Prophet's death some of his opponents, also claiming to be prophets, attempted to produce what they referred to as "revealed" texts, although the texts they produced were imitations of the Qur'ān. In the post-prophetic period even some Muslims claimed that they could compose at least the like of parts of the Qur'ān. Understandably, these texts were not well received by the Muslim community and were considered inferior to the Qur'ān, in both literary quality and artistic beauty. As to why people could not meet the challenge the Qur'ān poses, most Muslims appear to believe that, because the Qur'ān is God's word and has the perfection that can come only from God, human beings and jinn simply cannot compose such a perfect text. There were, however, Muslims (of the rationalist school of thought, the Mu'tazila) who held that human beings had the ability to produce a book like the Qur'ān but God simply prevented them from doing so.

The Inimitability of the Qur'ān

The ideas among Muslims as to why the Prophet's opponents and others could not produce a Qur'ān led to the development of a genre in Islamic tradition, during the ninth century CE, called the "inimitability of the Qur'ān" or *I'jāz al-Qur'ān*. Some scholars proposed that the Qur'ān was revealed through the Prophet Muhammad because he was "unlettered" (*ummī*) or, in other words, could not read or write. Muslim tradition has tended to underscore the idea that the Prophet could not read or write because it emphasizes the belief that the Qur'ān could not have been authored by someone like the Prophet if he was "unlettered."[2]

For Muslims, the Qur'ān is the most important, and for some, the only miracle attributed to the Prophet, although it mentions numerous miracles of Jesus, Moses, and of other Prophets. The miracle of the Prophet is in the inimitability of the Qur'ān. The Qur'ān is inimitable in a number of ways. It is matchless because its guidance is like no other. Muslims also believe that there is no other book in history that has had such a powerful impact on people's lives. The Qur'ān cannot be imitated in terms of its literary perfection either. For those who are familiar with Arabic, the Qur'ān is exceedingly beautiful in literary terms. It is also remarkably coherent, with clear continuity and consistency in its themes, even though it was revealed over a twenty-two year period. It would be difficult to author a text over that long and still retain the consistency and flow one finds in the Qur'ān, the argument goes.

In the modern period some new ideas have emerged among Muslims about the inimitability of the Qur'ān. For example, Rashad Khalifa (1935–90), a computer analyst, tried to demonstrate that the Qur'ān has an inherent mathematical code within it. According to his analysis, there is a close relationship between the letters and words of the Qur'ān and the number 19, which, Khalifa believed, is referred to in the words "Over it is nineteen" (74:30). Some Muslims also believe that the Qur'ān alludes to certain twentieth-century scientific facts and discoveries that could not have been known about during the lifetime of the Prophet. Muslims would argue that these aspects of the Qur'ān also point to the fact that it could not have been authored by another human being and could only have come from God.

In sum, the Qur'ān's self-perception is that no one other than God could have authored it. This confidence, in turn, has been translated into Islamic theology since the earliest centuries. Muslims' perception of their scripture, including its authenticity, accuracy, and reliability, has been heavily shaped by the Qur'ān's confidence in itself. However, this may have implications for how Muslims perceive other scriptures. Is the absolute confidence in the Qur'ān that underpins Islamic theology an obstacle to dialogue with other religious traditions? Does it necessarily lead to or result in the disparagement of other scriptures? Is it possible to develop an understanding of authenticity that does justice to the Qur'ān's perception of itself and the reverence it shows to the sacred texts of other religious communities? These are questions that need further thought and reflection.

Notes

1. In Islamic tradition, the word jinn is often used to refer to beings who are partly spiritual and are expected to worship God. They are not angels who, in Islamic tradition, do not have the power to disobey God, whereas jinn have the ability to disobey, much like human beings.

2. The Arabic word *ummī* can also be understood as meaning "coming from a community that does not have scripture," or as meaning that Muhammad was a gentile prophet, or from an uneducated people.

PART III

Methods and Authority in Interpretation

3.1 Authority in Interpretation
A Survey of the History of Christianity

JOHN LANGAN

In one of his Oxford University sermons, preached in 1843 at the church of St. Mary the Virgin, John Henry Newman spoke as follows:

> Thus St. Mary is our pattern of Faith, both in the reception and in the study of Divine Truth. She does not think it enough to accept, she dwells upon it; not enough to possess, she uses it; not enough to assent, she develops it; not enough to submit the Reason, she reasons upon it; not indeed reasoning first, and believing afterwards, with Zacharias, yet first believing without reasoning, next from love and reverence, reasoning after believing. And thus she symbolizes to us, not only the faith of the unlearned, but of the doctors of the Church also, who have to investigate, and weigh, and define, as well as to profess the Gospel; to draw the line between truth and heresy; to anticipate or remedy the various aberrations of wrong reason; to combat pride and recklessness with their own arms; and thus to triumph over the sophist and the innovator.[1]

This passage is a very interesting reminder of the human need for interpretation and of the need of religious communities for authoritative resolution of the conflicting interpretations that arise within them. In what follows I offer a brief overview of these themes in the history of Christianity.

First, however, we begin with some general observations about authority. Authority is a notion intrinsic to religion. It points us to a special weight, so to speak, that determines decisions, a weight in the depths of my life, deriving ultimately from God. Acknowledging this weight is, I suggest, one way to make sense of the attitude often expressed in contemporary Western culture that declares "I am spiritual but not religious." I suggest that this is an attitude that will admit to spiritual interests and preferences, but that is not happy to be called religious in the sense of being bound or weighed down by a commitment to accept or obey a particular authority.[2] This is a condition typical of many of our contemporaries.

Authority is that to which I bow or bend the knee; it is that which guides my action and my thought. Authority is also a notion that crosses the boundaries between different disciplines, as well as boundaries between different ways of life. It features in law and politics; it applies to organizations, corporations, and governments; it is a prominent theme in different areas of study and policy. Authority is a capability that is discriminatory; it is used to guide choice among alternatives. It is also discretionary; it is not fully captured in a formula or rule. It is also socially recognized and as such can be powerful. Authority is a practical, juridical notion, giving its holder the ability to act, to decide, to constitute things; but at the same time, it is also an epistemic notion; we very often rely on authority in making our judgments. It gives us sources and models for our thinking. It gives us assurance; it is a capability that can provide guidance to self and to others. It can be contrasted with power on the one hand and with anarchy on the other. Authority often conflicts with conscience. It evokes various reactions of obedience or disobedience, acceptance or rejection, critical scrutiny or evasion, rebellion or conformity. We often think of authority as a power to command and to forbid. And it has, if we scrutinize it, a rather ambiguous relationship to persuasion and argument. We encounter exercises of authority that do not appear to be supported by argument; we can also encounter exercises of authority that disdain to stoop to persuasion. Authority can be located in a person, an office, a body or assembly of persons, an institution, a document, a book, a tradition. It is a notion that has strong normative content to it, and it forms part of any comprehensive moral and social order.

We turn now from these general reflections on authority from the standpoint of moral and political philosophy to the more specific and very challenging question of the relationship between authority and Christianity. Here we have to start with the authority of God, Creator and Lord, source of law and ultimate judge, a being both transcendent and omniscient, one who prevails over the forces of evil and shepherds his people, and who is, at the same time, the ultimate source of all legitimate and appropriate authority. Next we encounter the authority of the word of God, the word that comes to the prophet, manifesting and affirming God's authority over the political order, specifically over the monarchy of Israel, but also over the world at large. This authority is then transferred to and exercised by prophets, priests, and kings in Israel who have their different styles and gifts. The books of Samuel in the Hebrew Bible give us a fascinating account of the tensions between prophetic and royal authority.

They are also connected with the different institutions characterizing the formative period of Israel's existence. Across these different institutions, all of which are marked by a religious character, there develops of course a plurality of forms of authority, giving rise to dramatic conflicts as well as to an ongoing search for the true interpretation of God's word. The resulting interpretations are not in all cases identical or harmonious.

Christians of course acknowledge the continuing religious authority of the Hebrew Bible. Going beyond this, they find at the heart of the New Testament the authority of Jesus. His authority is manifested in a range of ways, such as in his teaching "as one having authority" (Matthew 7:29) and in his miracles (see, for example, the healing of the paralytic at Mark 2:1–12). But the authority of Jesus is also seen in his anger at human sinfulness, greed, and insensitivity to the holy in the episode of the cleansing of the Temple (Mark 11:15–19), or again in his performing the role of humble servant, washing the feet of his disciples at his last meal with them (John 13:1–20). But this humble role is at the same time an authoritative example.

In the New Testament Jesus thus appears as both a bearer and exemplar of religious authority and a critic of abuses of religious authority. As Matthew observes at the end of the Sermon on the Mount: "Now when Jesus had finished saying these things, the crowds were astonished at his teaching, for he taught them as one having authority, and not as their scribes" (Matthew 7:28–29). He is also ultimately revealed as the source of religious authority. So at the end of Matthew's Gospel, Jesus says to the disciples: "all authority in heaven and on earth has been given to me" (Matthew 28:18) before sending them forth to make disciples of all nations. The New Testament as a whole serves as a modification and a critique of the religious authority of the Old Testament. This is put with particular force in the Sermon on the Mount, especially in the antitheses (Matthew 5:21–48), with their contrasting of what had been said in "ancient times" and what Jesus is now teaching in the new messianic situation. One of the questions that Christians have been inclined to raise, particularly in the twentieth century, is whether this is a model for the future development of Christianity or whether it represents a limit to the future development of Christianity. Thus some Christians have applied the model of Jesus's teaching here in a liberal or radical style, in effect saying that whereas Jesus taught certain things in his time, we are now free or are even required to teach something else. In contrast, other Christians have argued that, precisely because of his unique standing, Jesus is not to be surpassed and so his teaching constitutes a limit rather than a model to be freely applied.

The New Testament attests to ongoing contests of interpretation: debates over the relationship between faith and works; on the person, work and divinity of Christ; on the relationship of the Christian community to Judaism. In some cases we may only hear one side of these debates, but it is particularly clear from the passion that Paul brings to them that they were extremely lively and were far from being serenely dialogical. There is a continuing desire in the New Testament for continuity and authenticity of teaching: to teach as Jesus taught, to hand on what has been received, to maintain the unique and final status of Jesus, and to follow Jesus wherever he would go. But at the end of the story of the life of Jesus, as given to us in the Gospels, the disciples are empowered by the Holy Spirit. They move into a phase of life in the church in which there are many gifts that raise issues of authority and interpretation (1 Cor. 12).

We move on now rather rapidly from that early period of ferment and hopeful beginnings to the efforts to resolve fundamental issues of interpretation (particularly about the person and work of Christ) that constituted the Trinitarian and Christological controversies of the fourth and fifth centuries. A feature of those controversies that is of particular importance for the theme of this chapter is that the resolution of these conflicts of interpretation was undertaken by a council of bishops with imperial organization and support. This became the predominant way of settling crucial contests of interpretation within Christianity. Theologians and charismatic religious leaders, including monks and figures in a prophetic style, would arise from time to time and have an important influence on the life of the church, but conflicts of interpretation would ultimately be settled by the episcopal hierarchy. In this period we also find that a fundamental concern for orthodoxy as contrasted with orthopraxy became a strongly established and defining feature of the Christian community. This also became the basis for exclusion and division, with a move from reliance on scripture to a strong emphasis on creeds, which often introduced nonbiblical concepts.

In the East, reliance on episcopal resolution of problems led to pluriformity, the creation of autocephalous churches, and also, with the rise of Islam, to a loss of integration between episcopal leadership and political community. The West, meanwhile, saw the development of papal primacy, especially after the Gregorian Reform of the eleventh century. The interpretive community became effectively a body of scholars and theologians ruled by a papal monarchy that also had a very extensive agenda in church governance, and Italian and imperial politics.

In due course, the sixteenth-century Reformation presented a very broad challenge to this religious monarchical authority; at the same time, it also developed, in most of the emerging nation states of Western Europe, various forms of subordination of the religious to the political. Within the religious realm, scripture was taken to be supremely important in the Protestant world (*"sola scriptura"*) and itself became really the locus of saving truth and of authority. It was thought by at least some that the meaning of scripture was transparent to all believers, all men and women of genuine faith. Various mixed forms of church polity developed from the resolution of doctrinal and interpretive controversies. Coming out of the left wing of the Reformation, there emerged Baptist and other movements that really embraced what were in theory, if not always in practice, forms of religious anarchy. In the Protestant world, the Bible was declared to be authoritative, but the ongoing struggle to interpret it was entangled with the struggle to gain power and to set policy in the religious and political communities of the West. This was particularly manifest in the English Civil War in the mid-seventeenth century.

If we move on to the eighteenth and nineteenth centuries, separation between church and state began to be an explicit objective of significant thinkers and groups, and in most Western societies the authority of religion came to be restricted. Religion took on an increasingly marginal role in most cultural spheres and various forms of secularization were brought about through legislation and also through the impact of broader social and political movements. The same period also saw the rise of biblical criticism, which is a search for truth and meaning in interpretation, a form of knowledge that intertwines academic and religious communities with each other, and in which the dominant forms of authority are those of the academic community. There was also enormous growth in knowledge about the biblical world, with developments in Middle Eastern archaeology contributing to a vast increase both in the range of questions being asked about the Bible and also in the ability of scholars to provide at least partial answers to these questions. During this period, there was also increasing emphasis on the diversity of literary forms and the plurality of authorship in the Bible. Although these points had always been recognized to some degree, they now became much more important in the work of interpretation, which now began to move farther and farther from an insistence on the one divine author to a more fine-grained scrutiny of the complexities of the various human authors of the biblical books or sections thereof.

The growth of biblical scholarship of this kind created a distinct and more academic center of authority with regard to interpretation. This approach has been dismissed by various kinds of Christians of literalist, fundamentalist, and immutabilist outlook, including a fair number of Catholics. It has, however, been partially incorporated by official Catholic teaching, largely by means of a sharp distinction between issues of creedal importance, on which the papal and episcopal magisterium would settle matters, and issues outside that area of maximum concern and sensitivity, in which scholarly opinion could generally have free rein. There are continuing tensions in most Christian traditions between systematic and biblical theology; this has certainly been true of Catholicism. The historical-critical method was practiced and championed primarily by liberal Protestants, who, it is sometimes said, had the satisfaction (or surprise) of sawing off the branch on which they were sitting. In the wider intellectual world a very significant development in the last generation has taken place as changes in the philosophy and sociology of science have given rise to new perspectives on the concept of authority. There is now much more recognition of the role of tradition and of authority, with science being seen as much more of a social enterprise that manifests many of the same normative characteristics to be found in humanistic disciplines, in religion, and in other social enterprises.

This brief survey inevitably leaves many questions unanswered. Along with wide agreement on such issues as the ongoing need for interpretation (and indeed the inescapability of it), there are many unresolved and probably irresolvable disputes about various questions, such as: Who has authority with regard to interpretation? Precisely what principles will guide the decisions of these people with regard to interpretation? How will they integrate the academically relevant forms of knowledge into their decisions? How will the results of interpretation affect the wider activities of the faith community and civil society at large? A live question within some traditions (such as Roman Catholicism and Anglicanism) is whether religious leaders have too much or too little authority with regard to issues of interpretation. And, finally, a broader cultural question: If authority is seen as a form of power, and if one thinks along the lines of Lord Acton on the dangers of power, does authority inevitably corrupt those who hold it? It is very difficult in contemporary culture, with its strong anti-authoritarian tendencies, to give a positive account of the role of authority in society generally and in religion particularly.

Having acknowledged these difficult questions, before concluding I would like to make some suggestions about ways forward. Here I return to Newman, who in his 1845 *Essay on the Development of Christian Doctrine*, one of the great works in the intellectual history of the nineteenth century, affirms that development is a necessary feature of Christianity. The following short passage sets out his essential point:

> Again, if Christianity be an universal religion, suited not simply to one locality or period, but to all times and places, it cannot but vary in its relations and dealings towards the world around it, that is, it will develop. Principles require a very various application according as persons and circumstances vary, and must be thrown into new shapes according to the form of society which they are to influence. Hence all bodies of Christians, orthodox or not, develop the doctrines of Scripture.[3]

Whereas Newman's point here might be regarded as blindingly obvious in the academic world, in various religious communities it is still highly contested. Newman himself was tortured by the issues that he addresses in this book, the writing of which was in effect his bridge from Anglicanism to Roman Catholicism. One may not be persuaded by his argument for an infallible developing authority but Newman does offer some provocative observations on what he calls "notes of a genuine development." We need to recall that in Newman's time Catholicism was the pro-development party and Evangelical Protestantism was the anti-development party, and he was very concerned with the issues raised by the Protestant dismissal of change within Catholicism as deviation from the original revelation. He therefore attempted to define principles (or "notes") that would serve the process of discerning the difference between genuine developments and corruptions.

Newman's first "note of a genuine development" is "preservation of type." Here he makes use of the analogy of an oak growing from an acorn. Through the various stages of a plant's growth the character of what is developing is preserved, although the process of development may be accompanied by quite remarkable differences in physical appearance and scale. The second note, "continuity of principles," holds that there are certain core values that are really prior to doctrines and that shape the course of development. The further principles are: "power of assimilation"; "logical sequence"; "anticipation of its future"; "conservative action upon its past"; and "chronic vigour."

Although Newman proposed these principles as a means of dealing with some of the most fundamental, contested issues between Protestant and Catholic Christians, I see no reason not to apply them more widely to any tradition of ideas, religious or otherwise. For example, they might be applied to the workings of the US Supreme Court. In the context of Christian-Muslim dialogue it would be particularly interesting to reflect on their possible relevance not just to Christianity, but also to the historical development of belief and law in the Islamic world.

Notes

1. John Henry Newman, *Sermons Chiefly on the Theory of Religious Belief Preached before the University of Oxford* (London: Francis & John Rivington, 1844), Sermon 14, "The Theory of Developments in Religious Doctrine," preached February 2, 1843, 312–13.

2. "Religion" is derived from the Latin *ligare*, which means "to bind."

3. John Henry Newman, *An Essay on the Development of Christian Doctrine*, ed., Charles Frederick Harrold (New York: Longmans, Green and Co., 1949), 53.

3.2 Authority in Qur'ānic Interpretation and Interpretive Communities

ABDULLAH SAEED

Any discussion about authority in interpretation within the Islamic tradition begins with the centrality of God's word. God's word is not just another text but the direct speech of God (*kalām Allāh*). Indeed, the speech of God, addressing the Prophet, began with the word *iqra'*—"Recite!" (Qur'ān 96:1). God's word guides, advises, commands, prohibits, instructs, urges, rules, and encourages believers. It is the first and foremost authority in Islam, and is represented in the Qur'ān.

The Prophet Muhammad, the intermediary between God's word and the first community of Muslims, is both closely connected to the revelation of God's word and also its chief exponent. It was through him that God's word was revealed, and his exposition of the Qur'ān provided the basis for applying God's word in the first Muslim community in Mecca and Medina between 610 and 632 CE. The Prophet, therefore, is vested with the second most important authority in Islam, after the authority of God.

The faith of Muslims revolves around the revelation of God's word in Arabic. Indeed, the Qur'ān mentions in no less than ten verses that it was intentionally revealed in Arabic. For example, "We have sent it down as an Arabic Qur'ān" (12:2), and "Thus We have sent by inspiration to you an Arabic Qur'ān" (42:7).[1] The Qur'ān clarifies that this was because the Prophet was sent to an Arabic-speaking people: "We have sent no apostle but with the language of his people so that he might make the revelation clear to them" (14:4).

Even though God's word is represented in human language, not all of it is easily understandable (even for native speakers of Arabic) or lends itself always to clear interpretation. Within the Islamic tradition, Qur'ānic texts have generally been categorized according to the clarity of their meaning. Ibn 'Abbas, one of the first generation Muslims, famous for his contribution to understanding the Qur'ān, reportedly described four levels of texts in the Qur'ān: (1) texts whose meaning is known to the Arabs simply because of their command of Arabic; (2) texts whose meaning is known to all Muslims at a basic level, such as those that instruct Muslims to pray or fast; (3) texts whose meaning is known only to experts or scholars; and (4) texts whose meaning is known only to God.[2]

By delineating these categories, Ibn 'Abbas affirms that there are four levels of authority when it comes to interpreting the Qur'ān. These range from anyone with the necessary Arabic language skills; to all Muslims; to scholars; and finally to God. Similar views have been held by interpreters of the Qur'ān since the very early period of Islam.

The Qur'ān itself also recognizes that not all its texts can be interpreted easily. For example, 3:7 notes that some verses of the Qur'ān are difficult to interpret: "He has sent down this book, which contains some clear verses that are categorical and others allegorical, but those who are twisted in mind look for verses allegorical seeking deviation and giving them interpretations of their own. But none knows their meaning except God. And those who are steeped in knowledge affirm we believe in it, it is all from our Lord."

There have always been disagreements among Muslims as to which verses are categorical and which are allegorical. In an attempt to clarify this, some Muslim scholars have focused on the characteristics of each. For example, for some, categorical verses are those that have a clear meaning, do not require further explanation, and only have one meaning, which leaves no room for dispute. The verses of the Qur'ān that describe the prescribed (ḥadd) punishments (for theft and adultery) or what is clearly prohibited (ḥaram) or permitted (ḥalāl) for Muslims are seen as examples of categorical verses. Allegorical verses, on the other hand, are believed to be those texts whose meaning is not very clear or is known only to God. These are texts that have more than one possible meaning or that require further explanation, such as those verses that describe the attributes of God, what happens after death, and paradise and hell. Other interpretations of "categorical" and "allegorical" also exist in the tradition.[3]

Whatever the interpretation given to these two terms, Muslims throughout the centuries found that understanding God's word in Arabic was not easy. It was not simply a question of linguistic proficiency or knowledge of Arabic dialects that unlocked God's word. Knowledge of other areas and disciplines was necessary as well. Qur'ān 3:7 also makes the important connection between knowledge (referring to those who have in-depth knowledge) and interpretation of the Qur'ān. Elsewhere the Qur'ān also encourages Muslims to consult those who have knowledge about the word of God (16:43), and this knowledge can be both linguistic and contextual.

Interpretation during the Prophetic Period

Although interpretation of the Qur'ān was important for the first Muslim community of Mecca and Medina as they strove to understand and put into practice God's revelation, there is little evidence of the existence of extensive debates on Qur'ānic interpretation as a distinct and separate activity during the prophetic period. This may have been for several reasons. First, the Qur'ān was in Arabic and the Prophet and the first Muslim community were native Arabic speakers. Second, the social, political, intellectual, and cultural context of the Qur'ān was familiar to the first Muslim community. In fact, the context of the revelation was unfolding right before their eyes and the first Muslims were a living part of it. As such, the Prophet and the first community of Muslims were active in putting the Qur'ān into practice without any need to discuss or debate it. Understanding the Qur'ān during this period was therefore closely connected to Muslims' practice in context. This context, which was in fact an extension of the revelation, played a major role in facilitating understanding during the time of the first Muslim community.

Several aspects of the Prophet's context were important for understanding God's revelation: the time (610–32 CE) of the revelation; the place where it occurred (the Hijaz); the people to whom it was addressed (believers and others); the social, political, economic, and cultural norms and traditions of the Hijaz; and the existence of the Prophet at this time, as the chief exponent of God's word. It was the fusion of the Qur'ān, God's word, with this context that provided the foundation for what later came to be known as the most authoritative Qur'ānic interpretation.

Development of Authority in Qur'ānic Interpretation

While the Prophet Muhammad was alive there was little need to debate the issue of authority in interpreting the Qur'ān. The Prophet was alive and God's revelation came through him. If there was ever any doubt as to what the revelation meant, the Muslim community could call upon the Prophet, who was always ready to explain the message or to apply it to community needs. God's ever-present command and voice were more than enough to remind the believers that what was presented in the Qur'ān was the will of God, expressed in Arabic. It was only after the Prophet's death that competing personal opinions and interpretations of the Qur'ān became the norm. It was in this post-prophetic period of extreme fluidity that Muslims began to debate the issue of authority in interpretation.

After the death of the Prophet the situation changed dramatically. God's final revelation was now complete and the Prophet was no more, and within a short period of time, the political and cultural context of the Muslim community began to change as well. Politically, the Muslim community began to expand rapidly outside Arabia, drawing into itself new regions, cultures, and peoples. This in turn brought new cultural issues and problems for the Muslims to address. As there was no longer the Prophet to consult, the Muslims turned to the leaders of the community, the leading Companions of the Prophet, who assumed the role of mediators between the word of God and this new context. Given that these first leaders had lived with the Prophet, they were regarded as experts, thoroughly familiar with the context of the revelation and the revelation itself, and their judgments in the emerging new context held great authority for the Muslim community.

Over time, with the growing number of converts to Islam from other religions and the rising number of second and third generations of Muslims, endless debates began to emerge on important theological issues such as the definition of "Muslim," "non-Muslim," "believer," "unbeliever," "community," the nature of God, and the like. These early theological debates and competing views relied heavily on Qur'ānic texts for support.

Despite the fact that Qur'ānic texts were used as the basis of various theological positions, interpretations were highly contested. This was partly because no clear path, principles, or authority existed to settle debates on interpretation between Muslims. It took two to three centuries of debate and the existence of a multiplicity of personal opinions before broad, recognizable groupings formed within Muslim thought: religio-political groupings such as Sunnism, Shi'sm, and Kharijism; legal schools such as Maliki, Hanafi, Shafi'i, Hanbali, and Ja'fari; and theological schools such as the Ash'aris and Maturidis. Within each group, "mainstream" views developed alongside divergent, minority opinions. The interpretations and positions that were in line with mainstream thinking within each group eventually came to be regarded as "authoritative" for that group.

It is important to note that unlike the authority of God and the Prophet, which was more or less universally agreed upon within the Islamic tradition, the authority that emerged in the first few centuries in most interpretive communities was largely collective, not individual in nature. Individual scholars did have an important role; however, it was the collective authority to which individual scholars themselves were subject. This meant that within each interpretive community, be it religio-political, legal, or theological, Qur'ānic interpreters subjected their exegesis to the norms, rules, and principles of the broader mainstream community to which the interpreters belonged. For example, a Sunni interpreter of the Qur'ān belonging to the Maliki school of law, such as Qurtubi (d.1273), emphasized the Sunni-Maliki interpretive community's concerns. However, often interpretive communities overlapped in this regard, making the question of authority even more complex and multifaceted.

There has been one area of Qur'ānic interpretation, however, that is remarkably consistent within the Islamic tradition: the area of legal interpretation. For those Qur'ānic texts that are related to ethical-legal matters, interpretations have been very similar across interpretive communities. Legal interpretation has been dominated by the authority of the major legal schools or *madhhabs*, which set down clear lines of authority and principles of interpretation that have been highly influential.[4] In contrast, interpretation of the other text types lacked the same kind of consistency.

A number of scholars, however, attempted to work out ways of ensuring that the interpretation arrived at was at least reliable, if not authoritative, by insisting that the interpreter must have certain "qualifications." These included characteristics that the interpreter himself should possess in order for him to have the necessary individual authority to interpret the Qur'ān. The interpreter of the Qur'ān was expected: (a) to be "sound" in belief and hold orthodox theological positions; (b) to have excellent knowledge of the Arabic language, its grammar, syntax, morphology, stylistics, and the like; (c) to have excellent knowledge of a range of disciplines relevant to understanding the Qur'ān; (d) to have the necessary skills to comprehend the text; and (e) to avoid simply using his own opinion to interpret the text.

As the tradition of interpretation developed, three approaches emerged that were not quite comfortable with each other. First, a "text-based" approach, that involves a more faithful following of texts and tradition, particularly when it comes to interpreting legal and theological texts; second, a "reason-based" approach, characterized by greater liberty in exploration of the text and relying, to a high degree, on reason, particularly when it comes to theological texts; and third, a "mystical" approach, to be found within certain Shi'i and Sunni trends and particularly within Sufism, that searches for hidden meanings within the text.

Although each of these approaches exists in the tradition of Qur'ānic interpretation, there has been a remarkable emphasis, particularly within Sunni Islam, on the authority of a text-based approach to interpretation. That is, the closer you are to a Qur'ānic text and its meaning, particularly at the literal level, the safer you are and the more authentic your interpretation. Related to this is the belief that it is possible to arrive at an "objective" meaning of the text through a focus on a linguistic analysis of the text. The dominance of the text-based approach came about through the gradual decontextualization and objectification of God's revelation.

The Move from Context to Textual Authority

While the first Muslim community had access to the immediate context of the Qur'ān, later generations became increasingly removed from this immediate context—that is, the time and conditions of the Prophet and the first Muslim community. Thus later generations had to interpret God's revelation without the immediate experience or reference of the revelation, relying instead on second-hand texts, such as ḥadīth or *athār* (traditions), to gain a sense of the context of the Qur'ān. As God's revelation was compiled as a written text and naturally "removed" from the original environment in which it was revealed, the early Muslims had to treat it largely as a text. God's word became an object in itself to be studied and analyzed. Its understanding, which in the earliest period was closely connected to its immediate context, came to be gradually related to understanding the language of the text. Thus mastery of interpreting God's word in many cases came to be reduced to a mastery of the language of the text, and the immediate context of the revelation, which had played such a huge role in helping the earliest Muslims relate God's word to their life, became somewhat marginalized.

While there was some interest in Qur'ānic interpretation on issues like the occasions of revelation (*asbāb al-nuzūl*), mostly for legal reasons, there was little discussion of the broader context of the revelation, and no significant principles were developed to relate God's word to its immediate context. Instead, the concept of the universal applicability of the meaning of the text was developed without regard to the specific context in which the Qur'ān was revealed. The lack of interest in the broader context of the revelation has continued in the tradition right up to the modern period, a fact that continues to have a significant impact on modern debates on the interpretation of the Qur'ān.

Authority in the Modern Period

A growing number of Muslim voices are questioning whether the neglect of the context of the revelation, which has dominated Qur'ānic interpretation for centuries, and still largely does so, is appropriate. After all, how can the Qur'ān, which was revealed in seventh-century Arabia, relate to some of the concerns and needs of Muslims today if only linguistic principles are relied on for understanding its meaning without taking into consideration its socio-historical context? Although for some Muslims such questions should not even be asked, they have been raised by Muslim thinkers and movements from modernists and neo-modernists to feminists and progressive-ijtihadis, all of whom can collectively be described as "contextualists."[5] Their search for an appropriate methodology to apply the Qur'ān to contemporary concerns and needs has sparked a variety of new approaches to Qur'ānic interpretation. Much of this renewed interest in context has been directed toward the legal texts of the Qur'ān, as Muslim scholars and thinkers grapple with tensions between contemporary needs and the Qur'ān's teachings on a range of ethical-legal issues. These approaches, at their heart, inadvertently challenge the authority structures established over the course of the past 1,400 years.

In the modern period, particularly during the past century, the hold that various schools, both theological and legal, have had on Muslims has weakened significantly. This fragmentation of traditional authority structures has allowed a vast array of voices, interpretations, and arguments for change to arise. For example, the onslaught today of the Salafi movement, which advocates a "going back" to the time of the *Salaf,* or the earliest Muslims and their views on interpretation, has provided a strong basis for a more personal and individual authority in religious matters and interpretation, even though they would argue that they are calling for the reinstatement of the collective authority of the earliest Muslims.

For Salafis, it is relatively easy for a Muslim living in the twenty-first century to revert to the seventh-century texts without any need for the 1,400 years of scholarship and tradition to play any intermediary role. In their view the intellectual activities of the past centuries have only added to Muslims' confusion today about the "correct" interpretation of the foundation texts of Islam. For them, the best way to address this is by returning to the text of the Qur'ān and the ḥadīth of the Prophet, and possibly some views of the earliest authorities of Islam. By simply examining the language of these texts Muslims can arrive at a more objective meaning and thus understand how Islam was practiced in the early seventh century at the time of the Prophet. This view of course is under attack from non-Salafi scholars.[6]

In addition to the Salafis, a large number of other new groups have emerged today with interesting ideas about interpretation. These ideas of course are also challenging established norms, principles, and authorities in interpretation. Many Muslims today are beginning to challenge even legal scholarship and interpretation, an area that has not been disputed for a very long time. One notable example where this challenge is obvious is in the debates on gender equality, where an increasing number of scholars and Muslim feminists are challenging several rulings on women in classical Islamic legal texts and attempting to bring them in line with modern-day expectations and values. The classical interpretation of legal texts such as these has been regarded as almost immutable for centuries.[7] Even in the theological arena, issues that were supposed to have been resolved in early Islam and on which there was remarkable consensus are now being challenged. Examples include the relationship between Muslims and non-Muslims, how Muslims see other religions, and the question of freedom of religion.[8]

What is emerging from this very fluid contemporary environment is a number of interesting ideas, positions, and views. There is significant debate about the need to rethink key aspects of the idea of "revelation," particularly in order to emphasize the context of God's revelation and to identify what is universal and what is particular in the Qur'ān. The Muslims who raise such questions are not advocating a complete divorce from past traditions or the setting aside of past interpretations, but are arguing that serious consideration should be given to the context of the revelation at the time of the Prophet and the needs of people today in any interpretation of God's word.

These new ways of approaching interpretation of the Qur'ān should not be seen as problematic because authority in interpretation has always varied in Muslim tradition. The first few centuries of Islam, which were highly fluid, led to the emergence of a range of interpretive communities, and in the modern period Muslims are again functioning in such an environment. It has always been the case that different contexts have demanded different responses in relation to interpretation. Today's fluidity is likely to lead to the emergence of new interpretive communities, with fresh ideas on interpretation in relation to law, theology, and engagement with other religious traditions, to name but a few significant issues. The emerging authorities in interpretation may well be very different from those of the pre-modern period, but they will be just as valid and they will better equip Muslims to live out their faith in our contemporary world.

Notes

1. Translations of Qur'ānic passages are my own.

2. Abu Ja'far Muhammad b. Jarir al-Tabari, *Jāmi' al-bayān 'an ta'wīl ay al-Qur'ān* (Beirut, 1998), vol. I, 33.

3. Abdullah Saeed, *Interpreting the Qur'an: Towards a Contemporary Approach* (Oxon: Routledge, 2006), 109–10. For examples of a wide range of classical and modern Muslim interpretations of this key verse, see also Mahmoud M. Ayoub, *The Qur'an and Its Interpreters, Volume II* (Albany: State University of New York Press, 1992), 20–46.

4. For some discussion of this point see Kecia Ali, "Progressive Muslims and Islamic Jurisprudence: The Necessity for Critical Engagement with Marriage and Divorce Law" in Omid Safi (ed.), *Progressive Muslims: On Justice, Gender and Pluralism* (Oxford: One World, 2003), 163–89.

5. See, for example, Abdullah Saeed, *The Qur'an: An Introduction* (Oxon: Routledge, 2008), 219–32.

6. Abdullah Saeed, *Interpreting the Qur'an*, 102–15.

7. See, for example, Asma Barlas, *"Believing Women" in Islam: Unreading Patriarchal Interpretations of the Qur'ān* (Austin, TX: University of Texas Press, 2002); Amina Wadud, *Qur'an and Woman: Rereading the Sacred Text from a Woman's Perspective* (Oxford: Oxford University Press, 1992).

8. Abdullah Saeed, "The Charge of Distortion of Jewish and Christian Scriptures," *The Muslim World* 92 (3&4), Fall 2002, 419–36; Abdullah Saeed and Hassan Saeed, *Freedom of Religion, Apostasy and Islam* (Hampshire: Ashgate Publishing, 2004).

3.3 Reading Scripture in the Light of Christ

Matthew 12:1–8; Luke 24:44–49

SUSAN EASTMAN

Matthew 12:1–8

¹At that time Jesus went through the cornfields on the sabbath; his disciples were hungry, and they began to pluck heads of grain and to eat. ²When the Pharisees saw it, they said to him, "Look, your disciples are doing what is not lawful to do on the sabbath." ³He said to them, "Have you not read what David did when he and his companions were hungry? ⁴He entered the house of God and ate the bread of the Presence, which it was not lawful for him or his companions to eat, but only for the priests. ⁵Or have you not read in the law that on the sabbath the priests in the temple break the sabbath and yet are guiltless? ⁶I tell you, something greater than the temple is here. ⁷But if you had known what this means, 'I desire mercy and not sacrifice,' you would not have condemned the guiltless. ⁸For the Son of Man is lord of the sabbath."

Luke 24:44–49

⁴⁴Then he said to them, "These are my words that I spoke to you while I was still with you—that everything written about me in the law of Moses, the prophets, and the psalms must be fulfilled." ⁴⁵Then he opened their minds to understand the scriptures, ⁴⁶and he said to them, "Thus it is written, that the Messiah is to suffer and to rise from the dead on the third day, ⁴⁷and that repentance and forgiveness of sins is to be proclaimed in his name to all nations, beginning from Jerusalem. ⁴⁸You are witnesses of these things. ⁴⁹And see, I am sending upon you what my Father promised; so stay here in the city until you have been clothed with power from on high."

My colleague, David Steinmetz, wrote an essay about reading scripture called "Uncovering a Second Narrative," in which he compares reading the New Testament to reading a mystery novel.[1] Mysteries have complex plots with disparate events and characters, at the end of which the ingenious detective convenes all the characters in one room and retells the plot, drawing unexpected connections between characters and events, explaining how all has led to a particular conclusion, until—voilà!—the truth comes out. Something like this happens in the ways Israel's scriptures are taken up and resignified in relationship to Christ in the New Testament. The New Testament writers read scripture by starting at the end and reading backwards—that is, they find coherence and meaning through the revelation of Christ, who is the point of the story.

Whenever we read any text, we read from a certain vantage point in time and place. "Reading scripture in the light of Christ" means that we read from the time and place of the crucified and resurrected Christ. That is to say, we read scripture after the cross and the resurrection, with the expectation that Christ is its fulfillment and *telos*, its goal and perfection. We also read with the expectation that Christ is the final interpreter, as well as interpretation, of Israel's scripture. From the standpoint of Christian faith, we know Christ through the scriptures of Israel, but we also know those scriptures through Christ, who interprets them for us. Indeed, for Gentiles, it is through Christ that we have access to those scriptures. In addition, we know Christ through the new scripture that originates in his life, composed of his words and deeds, and interpreted through the complex life and witness of his followers. But more than this, and of utmost importance, is that to read from the place of Christ, in Christ, is to read with the expectation that Christ is present now, guiding our interpretation for the particularities of our time and place—which means to read in an attitude of prayer and waiting upon God.

The two texts considered here show us Christ interpreting scriptures of Israel, in different settings and different ways. In Matthew 12:1–8, Jesus disputes with the Pharisees over the interpretation and application of the Mosaic Law. In Luke 24:44–49, the risen Christ instructs his disciples immediately prior to his ascension. Taking these two passages in chronological order (both in the life of Christ and probably in the time of their composition), we will begin with Matthew.

First, whenever one reads Matthew, and particularly when one reads a dispute between Jesus and the Pharisees, it is important to situate this gospel in its historical context. The harsh polemic against the Jewish Pharisees in this gospel reflects, according to most scholars, the situation of a community of Jewish Christians who were painfully separating from the synagogue toward the end of the first century CE. The descriptions of Pharisees here are quite different from the ways in which Pharisees would have described themselves.

That said, disputes between Jesus and the Pharisees are common throughout Matthew, and as in this text, they always are about the interpretation of the Mosaic Law.

The passage immediately preceding Matthew 12:1–8 sets the crucial context for interpretation, and it is worth quoting in full:

> At that time Jesus said, "I thank you, Father, Lord of heaven and earth, because you have hidden these things from the wise and the intelligent and have revealed them to infants; yes, Father, for such was your gracious will. All things have been handed over to me by my Father; and no one knows the Son except the Father, and no one knows the Father except the Son and anyone to whom the Son chooses to reveal him. Come to me, all you that are weary and are carrying heavy burdens, and I will give you rest. Take my yoke upon you, and learn from me; for I am gentle and humble in heart, and you will find rest for your souls. For my yoke is easy, and my burden is light." (Matthew 11:25–30)[2]

Jesus promises deliverance for the common people from the "heavy burdens" of legal interpretation imposed on them by Pharisaic interpretations. "Yoke" refers to the "yoke of the law," which in the hands of Christ becomes easy. The story in the passage demonstrates this transformation. The dispute is over plucking grain—that is, doing work—on the Sabbath. In the context of the chapter, a second dispute immediately follows, this time over healing on the Sabbath and concluding with the interpretive principle, "It is lawful to do good on the Sabbath" (Matthew 12:9–12). In both cases, the matter at hand precisely concerns differing interpretations and hence applications of a shared text.

In the text here, the Pharisees complain to Jesus that, by harvesting grain on the Sabbath, his disciples are breaking the law. In fact, they do have a point. As W. D. Davies and Dale Allison observe, "Are not Jesus' followers neglecting a fundamental demand of the Decalogue? Are they not breaking a commandment God himself kept [at the creation]? Are they not doing away with one of the signs that separates Jew from Gentile?"[3] In support of the Pharisees' complaint, we can point to Exodus 34:21: "Six days you shall work, but on the seventh day you shall rest; in plowing time and in harvest you shall rest."

So the question is—is Jesus abrogating the law? I think not. Rather, he is arguing against a certain interpretation of the law, and he uses three references to scripture itself to do so. Each time he introduces his argument with a critique of the Pharisees' lack of understanding: "Have you not read?"—that is, have you not understood properly the meaning of the scripture? First he refers to a story from 1 Samuel 21:1–6, in which David (from whom the Messiah would come) "breaks the law" by eating the bread from the altar that only the priests could eat. Second, he refers to Numbers 28:9–10, where the priests in the temple are commanded to offer sacrifice on the Sabbath, thereby "profaning" the Sabbath. Here two authoritative examples, David the king and the temple priesthood, witness to the legality of the disciples' actions.[4] Finally, he concludes, "If you had understood" the words of Hosea 6:6, "I desire mercy and not sacrifice," you would not have condemned the guiltless.

Time precludes a full investigation of this passage, but I offer two brief observations. First, here we see Jesus giving an example of how to do biblical interpretation: he reads scripture in the light of scripture, and he reads all under the banner of the mercy of God. In doing so, he reads completely in line with the Law itself. It is crucial to remember that in Exodus 34:10–27, the renewal of the Decalogue, including the law of Sabbath observance, follows on the theophany to Moses in Exodus 34:6, where the character of God is revealed: "The Lord, the Lord, compassionate and gracious, slow to anger, and abounding in lovingkindness and truth." In the Septuagint, the second century BCE Greek translation of the Hebrew Scriptures, "gracious" is translated "merciful." It is the merciful character of God that resounds through Israel's scripture, and that grounds Jesus's interpretation of the Torah.

Second, not only does Jesus demonstrate how to interpret, through using other texts to interpret in line with God's mercy, he also demonstrates a peculiar authority over the meaning and application of the text. He does this through using a rabbinic method of reading called *qal wāḥōmer*, which is an argument from the lesser to the greater. In other words, "If A, how much more B." So Jesus says, in effect, that even David the king, and the priests in the temple, performed actions on the Sabbath, but something greater than the temple is here. How much more, then, does the Son of Man exercise authority over the Sabbath? In the next dispute over healing on the Sabbath, Jesus will use similar logic to argue for an interpretive principle based on mercy: if your sheep falls into a pit on the Sabbath, won't you pull it out? How much more valuable is a human being? "So it is lawful to do good on the Sabbath" (Matthew 12:12).

In the Matthew text, Jesus interprets the Mosaic law in reference to human behavior. Our second text comes from the last chapter of Luke, and focuses on the identity of Jesus. Here Christ's instruction to his disciples follows and summarizes three resurrection "appearances," and precedes Christ's ascension. As such, it looks both backward and forward, inviting us to do so also. As we turn our attention to what precedes this passage, we note that Jesus's words are the culmination of three stories in which he comes gradually into view, with much misunderstanding along the way on the part of the disciples. In each story, there is a pattern of appearance, nonrecognition, and further revelation.

The first appearance (Luke 24:1–12) is to the women who go to Jesus's tomb after the crucifixion, and it is not yet of Jesus himself. Rather, instead of finding Jesus's body as expected, the women meet two angelic messengers who say two significant things: First, "Why do you seek the living among the dead?" (24:5); second, "Remember what Jesus told you, while he was still in Galilee, that the Son of Man must be delivered into the hands of sinful human beings and be crucified and on the third day rise" (24:6–7). Already Jesus's life and words function as scripture, as the means of revelation and recognition. The women do remember Jesus's words and become the first witnesses of the resurrection. They return and tell the other disciples, who dismiss this as an idle tale (24:11).[5]

In the second appearance (Luke 24:13–35), Jesus joins two disciples as they are walking from Jerusalem to Emmaus, discussing these recent events. But he remains incognito. It is not simply that the disciples do not recognize him; rather, the text says, "Their eyes were kept from recognizing him" (24:16). The verb "were kept" is in the passive voice, leaving us to wonder who caused this inability to recognize Jesus. Usually in scripture the passive voice indicates God as the implied subject of the action, and as we shall see, such is the case here as well.

So Jesus falls in with the disciples, and he asks, "What is this conversation which you are holding with each other as you walk?" And "looking sad," they respond with what is surely one of the most ironic verses in all of scripture, "Are you the only visitor to Jerusalem who does not know the things that have happened there in these days?" No one was more personally involved in those events than Jesus himself! But he simply asks, "What things?" So they proceed to instruct Jesus on the events in his own life, culminating with the news of the women's vision of angels announcing that he was alive (24:17–24). Notice here how Jesus elicits from them their own version of events, and along with that, gives them the opportunity to express their own grief. The encounter is dialogical, so that when he does explain to them the truth of what has happened, their own lives are caught up into the narrative. In Jesus's interpretation of the scripture, they will see their own lives in a new light.

For it is through the scripture that Jesus explains the events that so trouble the disciples: " 'O foolish and slow of heart to believe all that the prophets have spoken! Was it not necessary that the Christ should suffer these things and enter into his glory?' and beginning with Moses and all the prophets, he interpreted to them in all the scriptures the things concerning himself" (24:25–27).[6] So now there are two sources of information: in the first encounter, we learn to attend to the words of Jesus himself; in this second encounter, our attention is directed by Christ to the scriptures concerning himself. Here Jesus not only interprets scripture; he is its content and meaning.

Nonetheless, the disciples still do not recognize him. It is only when he stays for supper, and takes the bread and pronounces the blessing, that "their eyes were opened, and they recognized him" (24:31). The verb is again in the passive voice, and its action speaks directly to the original condition of the disciples, when their eyes were prevented from recognizing Jesus. They could not fully recognize him of their own effort, even when he explained the scripture to them. Their eyes needed to "be opened," and this happens in the breaking of the bread. Jesus vanishes. In hindsight, in the light of their experience of him, the disciples ask each other, "Did not our hearts burn within us while he talked to us on the road and opened to us the scriptures?" (24:32). Jesus opened their eyes in the breaking of the bread, and he opened the scripture to them by interpreting to them the law and the prophets.

The third resurrection encounter (24:36–43) sets the stage for Jesus's words in the text. While the disciples share news of Jesus's appearance, he suddenly appears among them. Again, they do not recognize him immediately. But this time he demonstrates his identity by showing his hands and his feet, the scars of his crucifixion that demonstrate his continuity with the earthly Jesus. And further, he asks for something to eat—here is another meal in which he is made known. It is in this context that he again "opens" the disciples' minds to the meaning of the scripture about himself—his death and resurrection.

These three encounters present several points for our reflection. First, there is a pattern of appearance, nonrecognition, and then further revelation. This pattern is complicated by the use of passive verbs that attribute both blindness and sight to divine agency. Here God determines not only the content of revelation, but also the capacity to recognize that revelation. This is clear in the triple "opening" of the eyes, the scripture, and the disciples' minds through his interpretation of the scripture. Second, the angelic messengers remind the women of what Jesus himself taught, which in turn includes Jesus's own interpretation of Israel's sacred writings. Jesus's life generates revelation, even as he himself interprets the scriptures of Israel in a gradually encompassing way, starting with Moses and the Prophets, and then including the Psalms as well.[7] Therefore, the scriptures concern Jesus, and in particular the necessity of the Messiah's betrayal, death and resurrection. Luke's repeated use of "it was necessary"—*dei* in Greek—emphasizes that all this is according to God's plan.

Beginning with the angelic messengers' instructions to "remember," these stories direct our attention to the past in a way that gathers it up into God's action in the present. If continuity is about connection with the past, that continuity here is created and sustained by Christ's presence with his disciples. It is a gracious continuity that gradually brings Jesus into proximity with and recognition by the disciples who, after all, betrayed him. Perhaps they were not initially ready to meet him directly. The way of return is opened for them by Jesus's invitation to tell him their version of events, and then by his interpretation of the scriptures. Hence, the repentance and forgiveness that the disciples are to preach to all nations begins as good news for them personally.

But Jesus's final teaching of his disciples also directs their (and our) attention forward, both to the disciples' commission to be witnesses of Christ's death and resurrection, and also to the expectation of "the promise of the Father" (24:48–49). The promise of the Father is one of power from on high and we know, from the sequel to Luke in the Acts of the Apostles, that it refers to the outpouring of the Holy Spirit. But we don't see that promise fulfilled yet. It is of great importance that both the promise and the commission of the disciples are not realized by the end of this Gospel. The story is left open, to be continued in the ongoing life of Jesus's followers. By leaving the story open, Luke structures his Gospel so as to create a habit of expectation that God will continue to work and to be known in the life and mission of the apostles "to all the nations." Hence the interpretive work of Jesus's followers is not simply to read scripture and explicate its meaning, but to re-present his mission to all people. Interpretation is something that is worked out in the life of the community of faith.

Finally, this teaching of Jesus in Luke 24:44–49 is sandwiched between two references to Christ's physical absence from the disciples. First, after he breaks bread and pronounces a blessing on the two disciples he meets on the road to Emmaus, he vanishes from their sight (24:31). Second, after his final teaching, promise, and command, Jesus takes the disciples out to Bethany, blesses them, and again parts from them (24:51). So in this teaching, Jesus is making known to the disciples the ways he will be present with them now—in the breaking of bread, in the scripture, and in their fellowship with each other.

These two texts show Jesus interpreting scripture in two very different contexts. In Matthew, he explicates the meaning of the Mosaic Law as a guide to human relationships under the banner of divine mercy, and in reliance on his own authority. In Luke, the whole of scripture points to Christ's death and resurrection; yet that revelation requires the work of God in opening human understanding. In one sense, "reading scripture in the light of Christ" means, then, reading from the "end of the story," in which its meaning and coherence become clear. But in another sense, the story remains open, awaiting the further action of God.

These observations raise three questions for further reflection:

1. The way in which the disciples' eyes are "kept from" recognition and subsequently opened suggests that God is sovereign over unbelief as well as belief. This suggests in turn that to judge another's belief is to judge God. Is this idea of divine sovereignty over human comprehension present in Islam as well? How might it help us in matters of interfaith dialogue?

2. The dialogical quality of Jesus's interaction with his disciples suggests a dialogical quality in the interpretation of sacred texts. That is, as the meaning of the text is explicated, the meaning of our own lives is also revealed: we discover them implicated in the stories of the text. How does this "dual" revelation function in our respective traditions?

3. Jesus's commission of his disciples suggests that their interpretation of scripture will occur in their life together as much as their words. Interpretation is something to be enacted in the practices of the community. How are such interpretive practices worked out in our respective communities?

Notes

1. In Ellen Davis and R. Hays, eds., *The Art of Reading Scripture* (Grand Rapids, MI: Eerdmans, 2003), 54–65.

2. The biblical passages in this chapter are either from the New Revised Standard Version or are my own translations.

3. W. D. Davies, and D. Allison, *A Critical and Exegetical Commentary on the Gospel According to Saint Matthew*, Vol. 2 (Edinburgh: T & T Clark, 1988–97), 306.

4. Jesus follows good rabbinic practice here, posing a question followed by a scripture backing up his point. He also invokes two authoritative witnesses in his defense. In his confrontation with the Pharisees he uses familiar methods of exegesis and legal defense.

5. In some manuscripts, Peter runs to the tomb but also doesn't see Jesus and is left wondering.

6. The word translated "interpreted" is *diermēneusen*, from the root *hermēneuō*, "to explain, interpret," which is the source of the word "hermeneutics."

7. There is a gradually expanding picture of scripture in these narratives that accompanies the gradually expanding picture of Jesus: first, the words of Jesus; then, Moses and the Prophets; then "all the scriptures"; and finally, a threefold reference to the threefold division of the Hebrew scriptures: Moses (Torah), Prophets, and Psalms (the Writings).

3.4 Interpreting the Qur'ān
Qur'ān 3:7; 2:106; 16:101; 31:20

MUHAMMAD ABDEL HALEEM

3:7

It is He who has sent this Scripture down to you [Prophet]. Some of its verses are definite in meaning—these are the cornerstone of the Scripture—and others are ambiguous. The perverse at heart eagerly pursue the ambiguities in their attempt to make trouble and to pinpoint a specific meaning—only God knows the true meaning—while those firmly grounded in knowledge say, "We believe in it: it is all from our Lord"—only those with real perception will take heed.

["The cornerstone": literally "the Mother."]

2:106

Any revelation We cause to be superseded or forgotten, We replace with something better or similar. Do you [Prophet] not know that God has power over everything?

16:101

When We substitute one revelation for another—and God knows best what He reveals—they say, "You are just making it up," but most of them have no knowledge.

31:20

[People], do you not see how God has made what is in the heavens and on the earth useful to you, and has lavished His blessings on you both outwardly and inwardly? Yet some people argue about God, without knowledge or guidance or an illuminating scripture.

The passages selected for consideration here raise three issues that have been significant in the interpretation of the Qur'ān, with a great deal of discussion taking place about them in works of Islamic jurisprudence and *tafsīr*: the distinction between "definite" (*muḥkam*) and "ambiguous" (*mutashābih*)

133

verses (3:7); abrogation (*naskh*) (2:106 and 16:101); and the distinction between the "outward" (*ẓāhir*) and the "inward" (*bāṭin*) (31:20). These three issues will now be explored.

Muḥkam and *Mutashābih* (3:7)

Verse 7 speaks of two types of verses: *muḥkamāt*, which are readily understood and clear in themselves, and *mutashābihāt*, which do not have such clarity, and thus are open to more than one interpretation or view, literally "resembling one another," without decisive evidence for the intended meaning.

People who are "perverse at heart" do not occupy themselves with what is clear, the foundations (*al-muḥkam*), and eagerly seek or pursue the *mutashābih*, with the intention of causing trouble and confusion, and explaining it in a way to suit their own intentions.[1] In contrast, those "firmly grounded in knowledge" (not just faith) say, "We believe in it: it is all from our Lord," and they pray, "Lord, do not let our hearts deviate" (3:7–8).

There are two possible ways of reading the latter part of 3:7, bearing in mind that the Arabic text includes no punctuation. It is possible to pause after "God" (*allāhu*), in which case the meaning is "only God knows the true meaning"; the Arabic word *wa* is then translated as "while." But it is also possible to pause after "those firmly grounded in knowledge," in which case the meaning is "only God AND those who are firmly grounded in knowledge know the true meaning." This is just one case of ambiguity in the verse.

Al-Raghib al-Isfahani (d. 502/1109) divides the *mutashābihāt* into three types: verses whose meaning is known only to God, such as those concerning the time of the Last Hour; verses that require knowledge of the lexical meaning of words; and verses that can be understood only by learned people endowed with subtle perception from God.[2] Examples of *mutashābihāt* given by other scholars include: references to the timing of eschatological events; the meanings of the separate letters at the beginning of some sūras; and references to the attributes of God, which some see as anthropomorphic.

There are two approaches to dealing with the question of the divine attributes. The first is to believe in what is stated and leave its meaning to God. Imam Malik was giving a lesson one day, when a man referred to the words "The Lord of Mercy settled himself on the Throne" (20:5) and asked, "How

did God settle Himself on the throne?" The Imam sensed that this was a troublemaker, so he said, "The concept of settling oneself is known to all, but how
God did it is unknown. To believe in it as it is, is part of the faith; to question
it is a deviation. Get this troublemaker out of here!"[3] The second approach is
to take references to divine attributes as figures of speech. Thus the "hand" of
God (48:10) is taken to mean His help or protection.[4] Razi (d. 606/1209)
explains that such anthropomorphic descriptions of God are given to suit the
comprehension of common, lay individuals who would be baffled if given
abstract descriptions suitable only for erudite scholars. So they are given concrete terms, safeguarded by such other verses as, "There is nothing like Him"
(42:11).[5]

The pursuit of *mutashābih* has always been a source of trouble or difficulties
among Muslims, especially with those who seek to reinterpret the Qur'ān for
their own purposes. Even extremist interpretations can be seen as resorting to
such methods. In fact, taking verses out of context can cause them to become
mutashābih.

Naskh

Naskh is normally translated as "abrogation." The two verses, normally cited in
connection with this concept (2:106 and 16:101), are given in full at the start of
this chapter. Verse 2:106 is the only verse that includes a word derived from
naskh, so not surprisingly it is the one most cited. However, a strong challenge
was raised as to whether the verse refers to abrogation within the rulings of the
Qur'ān and whether it is in fact as relevant to Islamic law as it was later to
become. Abu Muslim (d. 322/933) denied that this verse referred to *naskh*
within Islam and held the view that it referred to the abrogation of Jewish, not
Islamic, rulings. Examination of the context of the verse strongly supports this
view. Long sections before and after it are concerned with the Jews and their
relations with the Muslims, as, for example, at 2:105: "Neither those of the
People of the Book who disbelieve nor the idolaters would like anything good
to be sent down to you [Muslims] from your Lord, but God chooses for His
grace (*raḥma*) whoever He will. His bounty (*faḍl*) has no limits." *Raḥma* and
faḍl here refer to the prophethood of Muhammad, which the Jews in Medina
begrudged (see also 2:109, 3:73–4, and 4:54). Following this, 2:106 emphasizes

that if God has "abrogated" any revelation, He always replaces it with something better or similar. The claim that 2:106 refers to changing rulings within the Qur'ān fails to do justice to the context.

What is *naskh*? Is it really abrogation? As will be seen, many of the examples cited as *naskh* are not abrogation per se. There is also the problem of the context of 2:106. Abu Muslim, who was followed by Muhammad Asad in our time, argued that the context of the verse is the long section concerned with the Children of Israel and that it therefore refers to the message of Muhammad superseding the message of Moses.[6] If this is the case, it cannot mean "complete abrogation" since much of what is in Moses's message is still present in the Qur'ān, which says it comes to "confirm" the essential Torah, rather than "abrogate" it (3:3, for example). The context of 16:101 involves not the Jews, but rather the Meccan idolaters, who "have no knowledge" (i.e., no scripture), and who argued that the Prophet was "just making up" what is in the Qur'ān—one of many such arguments used against him (21:3–5; 25:4–5; 52:29–33).

Despite all the ambiguities in these two texts, they have been relied on for the notion of *naskh* in the Qur'ān. In jurisprudence *naskh* has been defined as "lifting a Sharī'a ruling and replacing it with another, later one."[7] The wisdom behind this process was the intention to introduce legislation gradually, paying regard to the circumstances during the lifetime of the Prophet. The most frequently quoted example is the gradual prohibition of intoxicating substances (*khamr*), through the following four stages:

1. We give you a drink . . . From the fruits of date palms and grapes you take sweet juice [intoxicants (*sakaran*)] as well as wholesome provisions. (16:66–67)
2. They ask you [Prophet] about intoxicants and gambling: say, "There is great sin in both, and some benefit for people: the sin is greater than the benefit." (2:219)
3. You who believe, do not come anywhere near the prayer if you are intoxicated. (4:43)
4. Intoxicants (*khamr*) and gambling, idolatrous practices, and [divining with] arrows are repugnant acts—Satan's doing: shun them so that you may prosper. . . . (5:90)

It was kind and wise not to confront the new community of believers from the beginning with a complete prohibition, but the important thing to note here is that none of the "earlier" verses could be said to have been completely abrogated; they still apply.[8] In fact, it was the existence of such verses, more than the questionable application of 2:106 and 16:101, that gave rise to the discussions about *naskh*.

All jurists agree that *naskh* is not *badā'*; that is, something occurring to God that He did not know before. It is the extent of *naskh* that is the biggest issue here and on this question three trends can be identified. One approach, of which Abu Muslim is the main proponent, is to deny *naskh* completely. Another approach is to be extreme in applying it; this trend is exemplified by Ibn Salamah (d. 410/1019), who claimed, for instance, that the so-called "sword verse" (9:5) had abrogated 124 verses. He was contradicted even by his own daughter on one occasion when he commented on the verse that praised believers for giving the food they love to the poor, the orphans, and the captive (76:8). He had said that this had been abrogated in the case of non-Muslim captives by the "sword verse" but later conceded that his daughter was right.[9] Finally, there is the moderate view exemplified by al-Suyuti (d. 911/1505), who reduced the number of abrogated verses to nineteen. Others after him reduced the number further to ten; even these could be further reduced to perhaps three.[10]

Two important aspects of the classical understanding of *naskh* should be borne in mind. First, it emphasized that *naskh* could only happen during the time of the Prophet, while the revelation was still being received. Second, the principle of *naskh* could be applied only to Sharī'a rulings, not to matters of faith or ethics or any information given in the Qur'ān, nor indeed to Sharī'a rulings that have specific statements in the Qur'ān or Ḥadīth attesting to their permanency.[11]

Numerous examples can be given of exaggerated claims of *naskh*. For instance, some have divided very short verses into sections, claiming that one section abrogates another, even if it is in the very same verse, revealed at the same time. For example, in 9:5, Ibn Salama considers that the first clause, "kill [the polytheists] wherever you find them," has been abrogated by the end of the verse, "but if they repent and perform the prayer and pay the prescribed alms, let them go their way."[12] Other such examples include claiming that the termination of pre-Islamic practices (i.e. non-Sharī'a practices), such as marrying one's stepmother, was a case of *naskh*; every verse advocating giving to charity is abrogated by the institution of compulsory *zakat*; and the injunction to "speak good words to all people," given to the Children of Israel centuries before the time of the Prophet (2:83), had been abrogated by the "sword verse" (9:5) that refers to the people of Arabia who had broken their treaty with the Prophet. A final example is Ibn Salama's claim that the "sword verse" abrogated the *"jizya* verse" (9:29), even though *jizya* is part of the established Sharī'a law.

These examples all illustrate the state of wild speculation into which the question of *naskh* descended over several centuries, pushing some to go in the opposite direction and deny the validity of the very concept of *naskh*. However, the majority of jurists agreed with Al-Suyuti's middle way between denying it, like Abu Muslim, and going to the speculative extremes of populist preachers like Ibn Salamah.[13] This moderate majority tried to impose limits to such speculation by specifying the conditions for determining *naskh*. They insisted that there should be either clear textual authority for *naskh* from the Qur'ān or the sound Ḥadīth, or the consensus of all Muslim scholars, or, in the case of explicit contradiction that can be resolved by the mechanism of *naskh*, the certainty that one verse came after the other. Where such certainty was not available, *naskh* could not operate.

Ẓāhir and *Bāṭin*

The verse I was asked to discuss under this section is (31:20). However, this verse simply refers to God's blessings, both obvious, as seen around us (*ẓāhir*), and hidden (*bāṭin*), including whatever lies under the earth, or the smooth functioning of our inner organs and talents. I have consulted the Qur'ān concordance and found no evidence of the word *bāṭin* having any esoteric meaning or interpretation. It is crucial to note that whereas the concepts of *mutashābihāt* and *naskh* are supported by Qur'ānic texts, there is no such textual basis for a *bāṭinī* or esoteric approach to interpretation of the Qur'ān. The word *al-bāṭin* as a masculine singular is only used once referring to God, who is *al-Ẓāhir wa-l-Bāṭin* "the Manifest and the Hidden" or "the Outer and the Inner" (57:3). The only other use of *bāṭin* is at 6:120: "Avoid committing sin, whether openly [*ẓāhir*] or in secret [*bāṭin*]." Nor do we find in Wensinck's Concordance of Ḥadīth any reference to *bāṭin* suggesting esoteric interpretation.

In his monumental work on Islamic jurisprudence, *al-Muwāfaqāt fī uṣūl al-shārī'a*, the distinguished Andalusian legal scholar, al-Shatibi (d.790/1388), begins his discussion of *ẓāhir* and *bāṭin* by commenting, "Some people claim that the Qur'ān has *ẓāhir* and *bāṭin*," and then sets out to refute their claims.[14] He has his own explanation of what constitutes valid *bāṭini* interpretation. In sūra 110, God addresses the Prophet, saying, "When God's help comes, and He opens up your way, when you see people entering God's faith in crowds, celebrate the praise of your Lord and ask His forgiveness: He is always ready to accept repentance" (110:1–3). On hearing this, Ibn 'Abbas said that God here announces to the Prophet his imminent death. The same is said of God's statement in the passage revealed during the Prophet's Farewell Pilgrimage, "Today I have completed your religion for you" (5:3); again Umar wept and understood that these words meant the imminent death of the Prophet. This, for al-Shatibi, represents a valid *bāṭini* interpretation, which here refers to what is implied in the statement, but does not contradict the *ẓāhir*, the obvious meaning of the words.[15]

In response to the verse "Who will give God a good loan, which He will multiply for him?" (2:245) some Jews are reported to have said, "God is poor and borrows money while we are rich!" This is seen as *ẓāhir*, whereas a companion, on hearing this, said, "How generous God is, to give us money and then ask us to lend some of it back to Him in charity!" This is seen as *bāṭin*.[16] Shatibi sets two important criteria for any *bāṭini* interpretation: (1) that it is still valid according to the *ẓāhir* meaning of the Arabic wording that Arabs in their language consider to be the meaning, since the Qur'ān is Arabic; and (2) that it must have supporting evidence, testifying to its validity, that is explicit in another place, without anybody refuting it.[17]

Shatibi goes on to cite examples of the *bāṭinī* meanings claimed by some Isma'ili supporters of this doctrine, such as their teaching that fasting means "refraining from divulging secrets"; the five daily prayers means the Isma'ili four principles plus the Imam 'Ali; *ṭahāra* (cleanliness) is to purify oneself from any belief except following the Imam; Moses's staff means his argument that refuted the spurious arguments of the magicians; the parting of the sea means Moses's distribution of his knowledge among his followers; and the sacrifice of Isaac means Ibrahim making a covenant with him. In view of the criteria he stipulated, mentioned above, it was only natural that Shatibi rejected such interpretations.[18]

Shatibi gives a further type of interpretation that could be legitimately called *bāṭini*, taking some examples from the Sufi, Sahl al-Tustari (d. 283/896). Commenting on "Do not set up rivals to God" (2:22), Tustari said that the biggest rival is the soul that tempts you to commit evil and to yield to its demands without any guidance from God. Shatibi states that Tustari did not claim that this was a *tafsīr* of the verse, but that he had identified something that can be considered a rival to God, without cancelling the original meaning.[19]

Another example of what Shatibi considered *bāṭin* is the spirit of the law as opposed to the letter of it. Thus a husband who pressures his wife to make her give him money to divorce her, thinking that this is lawful because the Qur'ān allows payment, is not aware that somewhere else in the Qur'ān it says that the wife has to be willing to part with the money.

Shatibi makes some very interesting points in his attempts to distinguish between what does and what does not constitute valid *bāṭini* interpretation. However, the fact remains that in the Qur'ān the word *bāṭin* does not have any esoteric significance.

Notes

1. Shortly before this verse the Qur'ān warns "those who deny God's revelations" that they "will suffer severe torment" and that He is aware of what they do—"nothing . . . is hidden from Him" (3:4–5). This is echoed in verse 7: God is aware of what the perverse at heart do; their attempts to find problems with the scripture are an indication of disbelief.

2. Al-Raghib al-Isfahani, *Mu'jam mufradāt alfāẓ al-Qur'ān* (Beirut, 1972), on *mutashābih*.

3. Jalal al-Din al-Suyuti, *al-Itqān fī 'ulūm al-Qur'ān* (Cairo, 1941), vol. 2, 8.

4. Razi, *al-Tafsīr al-kabīr* (Beirut, n.d.), vol. 2, 87.

5. Cited in Zurqani, *Manāhil* (Cairo, 1954), vol. 2, 193–4.

6. Abu Muslim bin Bahr, reported by Razi, *Tafsīr*, vol. 3, 229; Muhammad Asad, *The Message of the Qur'an* (Gibraltar : Dar al-Andalus, 1980), 23, n.87.

7. M. H. Kamali, *Principles of Islamic Jurisprudence* (Cambridge: Islamic Texts Society, 1991), 149.

8. Thus the intoxicants are disapprovingly contrasted with what is wholesome; the prohibition against praying while drunk still applies.

9. Hibat Allah Ibn Salama *al-Nāsikh wa-l-mansūkh* (Beirut, 1986), 191.

10. M. Sh. Lashin, *al-La'āli' al-ḥisān* (Cairo, 1982), 210–12.

11. See A. Khallaf, *'Ilm uṣūl al-fiqh* (Cairo, 1977), 224–32.

12. Ibn Salama, *al-Nāsikh wa-l-mansūkh*, 94–5. This verse has been discussed at length in M. Abdel Haleem, *The Sword Verse Myth*, Occasional Paper 1, *Journal of Qur'anic Studies* 2007.

13. A. Khallaf, *'Ilm uṣūl al-fiqh* (Cairo, 1977), 224–75.

14. Shatibi's views have had profound effects on modern Islamic scholarship, especially since his book was edited by a prominent Azhari, Sheikh Abdallah Draz, and became part of

the curriculum of Al-Azhar, which gave them circulation throughout the Sunni Muslim world through its students.

15. Al-Shatibi, *al-Muwāfaqāt fī uṣūl al-sharī'a* (Beirut, 1975), vol. 3, 384.

16. Ibid., 388.

17. Ibid., 394.

18. Ibid., 394–95.

19. Ibid., 397–98.

3.5   The Use of Scripture in *Generous Love*

MICHAEL IPGRAVE

Michael Ipgrave's essay is printed after the following selection of passages (sections 1, 3, and 7) from *Generous Love: The Truth of the Gospel and the Call to Dialogue: An Anglican Theology of Inter Faith Relations*, prepared by the Anglican Communion Network for Inter Faith Concerns and published early in 2008.[1]

1   Beginning with God

Whenever as Christians we meet with people of different faiths and beliefs, we do so in the name and the strength of the one God who is Lord of all. Addressing the pagan Athenians, the apostle declares that this God is the One in whom all human beings live, move and have their being; he is the One of whom all can say: 'He is not far from every one of us'. [1] We cannot measure the infinity of God's greatness nor exhaust the mystery of his being; the religions of humanity deceive themselves when they fail to acknowledge the limits of their knowledge.

We believe that through the life, death and resurrection of Jesus of Nazareth the One God has made known his triune reality as Father, Son and Holy Spirit. The boundless life and perfect love which abide forever in the heart of the Trinity are sent out into the world in a mission of renewal and restoration in which we are called to share. As members of the Church of the Triune God, we are to abide among our neighbours of different faiths as signs of God's presence with them, and we are sent to engage with our neighbours as agents of God's mission to them. Thus,

We seek to mirror the Father's generous love.

The God who has created our world is generous in grace and rejoices in diversity—'O Lord, how manifold are your works! In wisdom you have made them all!'[2] He has created all men and women in his image, and he wishes all to enjoy that fullness of life in his presence which we know as salvation.[3] God cares for each person with a parental love; called to be perfect as our Father is perfect,[4] we know that we must show that same love and respect to all.

We proclaim Jesus Christ as the one who shows us God's face.

Jesus Christ the Son of God shows us 'the radiance of God's glory.'[5] He opens for us the way to the Father and we wish others to walk that way with us; he teaches us the truth which sets us free, and we wish to commend that truth to others; he shares with us his risen life, and we wish to communicate that life to others.[6] Our witness to Jesus as Lord must be attested by Christlike service and humility[7] if it is to be heard and seen by our neighbours as the good news of the Kingdom.

We celebrate the work of the Holy Spirit made known through the fruit of the Spirit.

It is not for us to set limits to the work of God, for the energy of the Holy Spirit cannot be confined. 'The tree is known by its fruits',[8] and 'the fruit of the Spirit is love, joy, peace, patience, kindness, generosity, faithfulness, gentleness and self-control.'[9] When we meet these qualities in our encounter with people of other faiths, we must engage joyfully with the Spirit's work in their lives and in their communities.

3   Shaping Anglican Insights: Reading the Scriptures

The Bible has primacy in Anglican theological method, in that we seek to be a community living in obedience to Jesus Christ, the eternal Word of God who is revealed through the words of Holy Scripture. In identifying the message of the Bible for the present, the Anglican method brings the insights of tradition and reason to the interpretation of the text in the light of experience. Our presence in, and engagement with, multireligious contexts lead us to read the Scriptures in new ways. We come to recognise that the people of God have already known and grappled with the challenges and opportunities of living amid religious plurality, and that those experiences have shaped the formative texts of Scripture. Thus, Israel worshipped the one Lord their God amongst the nations of the Ancient Near East, each following their own god; the first followers of the Way confessed the name of Jesus amidst the many philosophies and cults of the Roman Empire, and within the kingdoms to the east of that Empire. As the people of God today, we can find the biblical text coming to life in a new way as we engage in our discipleship with issues which raise questions similar to those they faced. For many in our Communion, the Bible speaks with immediacy and clarity into their contemporary situations of inter-religious encounter.

Many passages of the New Testament testify to the passion and persistence with which the first Christians struggled to understand their place within God's purposes for his people Israel. Whether Jews or Gentiles, they all believed that God had decisively and finally revealed himself in the person and work of the Jewish Jesus of Nazareth, and it was that conviction which gave such intensity to their efforts to understand the theological significance of Jewish law and religion and the Jewish people. Out of the rich and complex texts which record those efforts there have grown different ways of understanding Christian-Jewish relations in the history of the Church. 'A right understanding of the relationship with Judaism is fundamental to Christianity's own self-understanding';[10] as we seek guidance in this important area today, we need to recognise the continuing vitality of Jewish life and religion over the last two millennia. We must 'reject any view of Judaism which sees it as a living fossil, simply superseded by Christianity'.[11]

Our Scriptures speak to us in new ways when they are brought alongside the sacred texts of other religions in the practice known as 'Scriptural Reasoning'.[12] For example, believing ourselves to be in a dialogue with God enabled through the words of the Bible, it can be a profoundly humbling and creative experience for us to read the Bible alongside Muslims who likewise believe themselves to be addressed by the one God through the text of the Qur'ān. Hearing the stark divine imperative that 'You shall not bear false witness against your neigh-bour',[13] and recognising the spiritual profundity of parts of the Hindu scrip-tures, we can ponder how often we collude with a distorted view of the other if we dismiss Hinduism as merely polytheistic idolatry. Treasuring the 'read, mark, learn, and inwardly digest'[14] which our own Anglican spirituality com-mends in relation to the Scriptures, we can be challenged by the prolonged and intense attention which Buddhist tradition teaches as necessary for the sutras to become an interior reality. Set alongside the scriptures of other religions too, and the orally transmitted texts of other traditions, reading the Bible in these fresh contexts can both motivate and challenge us for engagement with people of different faiths.

7 Practising the Embassy and Hospitality of God

As God both pours out his life into the world and remains undiminished in the heart of the Trinity, so our mission is both a being sent and an abiding. These two poles of embassy and hospitality, a movement 'going out' and a presence 'welcoming in', are indivisible and mutually complementary, and our mission practice includes both.[15] In the Gospel Jesus teaches his disciples to deliver their embassy within the setting of receiving hospitality: 'Whatever house you enter, first say, "Peace to this house".'[16] As disciples we have to learn to be guests, and the proclamation we make in our embassy is in the first place the blessing of peace, the announcement of the good news of the Kingdom, and the healing of the sick. As ambassadors of Christ, our mission is to meet, to greet, and to acknowledge our dependence on other people and on God: 'We do not proclaim ourselves; we proclaim Jesus Christ as Lord and ourselves as your servants for Jesus' sake'.[17] The embassy which has been entrusted to us is the ministry of reconciliation,[18] and the giving and receiving of hospitality is a most powerful sign that those who were strangers are reconciled to one another as friends.

The Bible is full of images which point to the theological depth of the host-guest relationship. As God's people, we meet the test of hospitality when we offer the best provisions we have to the unexpected visitor, and still more through the time and care we give to addressing our guests' weariness and thirst.[19] We will do that out of the integrity of our Christian faith and practice; true hospitality is not about concealing our convictions, but about expressing them in a practical way. We ourselves can in turn receive in friendship the hospitality of others, which may speak powerfully to us of the welcoming generosity that lies at the heart of God. Through sharing hospitality we are pointed again to a central theme of the Gospel which we can easily forget; we are re-evangelised through a gracious encounter with other people.

The challenges to the practice of hospitality are many and serious. Our guests may be suspicious, fearful, or hostile, as we may be when we are guests. There may always be failures to reciprocate on either side. It is possible to use the practice of hospitality, not truly to accept and to recognise one another, but rather to suppress difference through a superficial bonhomie. We have to learn that being embarrassed, perplexed and vulnerable may be part of our calling as both guests and hosts, for it is when we welcome one another in all our differences that we are truly enriched by one another.

Hospitality is strengthened through the always time-consuming, often costly, and sometimes painful process of building trust. As that trust develops, sharp distinctions between host and guest may fall away, as they do at any convivial meal. We come to learn that the spaces in which we meet one another do not ultimately belong to either host or guest; they belong to God, as do the so-called 'neutral' spaces of public life. None of the places, situations or societies where we meet and greet are the exclusive territory of any one group; they are entrusted by God to be shared by everyone, since all humans are made in God's image.

Anglican spirituality maintains that at the heart of our life as a Christian community is a meal for those who know themselves to be strangers and pilgrims upon earth. At the breaking of the bread our Lord himself came to his disciples as one at first unknown.[20] The Eucharist opens us to an awareness that we too are guests of the Father waiting for the completion of his loving purposes for all. As he strengthens us with bread for the journey to carry us to that place which is a home for all the nations of the world, so here we share our life with our neighbours of all faiths as citizens of our earthly kingdoms. We wait for the day when all humanity together will meet the one divine host, the Father who invites all his children to share the joy of the banquet he has prepared.

Notes

1. Ac 17 27–28. St Paul indeed goes on to cite the words of the poet Aratus: 'For we too are his offspring.'

2. Ps 104.24.

3. 1 Tim 2.4.

4. Mt 5.48.

5. Heb 1.3.

6. Jn 14.6.

7. 2 Cor 4.5.

8. Mt 12.33.

9. Gal 5.22f.

10. *Jews, Christians and Muslims: The Way of Dialogue* (commended for study by the Lambeth Conference 1988), §13.

11. *Ibid.*, §16.

12. Scriptural Reasoning is 'a practice of group reading of the scriptures of Judaism, Christianity, and Islam that seeks to build sociality among its practitioners and release sources of wisdom and compassion for healing our separate communities and for repair of the world' (Steven Kepnes, 'A Handbook for Scriptural Reasoning', p.23, in David F. Ford and C. C. Pecknold, ed., *The Promise of Scriptural Reasoning*, (Oxford: Blackwell, 2006); also posted on

the *Journal of Scriptural Reasoning* website, http://etext.lib.virginia.edu/journals/jsrforum/). The practice has its origins in dialogue between Jewish and Christian scholars.

13. Ex 20.16, Dt 5.20.

14. *Book of Common Prayer*, Collect for the Second Sunday in Advent.

15. *Embassy, Hospitality and Dialogue: Christians and People of Other Faiths* – Report to the 1998 Lambeth Conference by Bishop Michael Nazir-Ali, posted on www.lambethconfer ence.org/.

16. Lk 10.5–9.

17. 2 Cor 4.5.

18. 2 Cor 5.20.

19. Gen 18.1–15, Heb 13.2.

20. Lk 24.16.

*   *   *

Background and Status

Generous Love: The Truth of the Gospel and the Call to Dialogue is a document prepared for the Anglican Communion by the Network for Inter Faith Concerns. As its subtitle, *An Anglican Theology of Inter Faith Relations*, indicates, *Generous Love* is intended to provide a brief synthesis of reflection within the Anglican Communion over the last forty years on the theological presuppositions and implications of Christian engagement with other people and communities of faith. It was drafted, through an extensive process of consultation, as a recognition of the fact that, despite the great growth of interest in the area over the last twenty years, no substantial international Anglican statement on inter faith relations had been produced since the 1988 Lambeth Conference document *The Way of Dialogue*. Moreover, *Generous Love* builds on the foundations established by *Nostra aetate* more than forty years ago, and other significant ecumenical work in this area; it seeks to integrate this growing corpus of theological reflection into a recognizably Anglican method.

Generous Love, like other Anglican Communion documents, has no normative or definitive status as a theological statement, but does carry value as a teaching resource that was studied by Anglican bishops at the 2008 Lambeth Conference, and disseminated by them to their dioceses. It is commended for study by the Anglican Consultative Council, and prefaced with a foreword by the Archbishop of Canterbury. Following its reception by the bishops at Lambeth, it can be seen as accepted by the bishops at Lambeth; it will become an agreed reference point for Anglican teaching on inter faith relations.

Structure and Themes

The argument of *Generous Love* is developed in eight short chapters, three of which are presented above. "Beginning with God" (1) sets out an account of God as one whose love goes out in restoration and renewal into the world that he has made, and who invites his people to share in that venture. The final chapter, "Sending and abiding" (8), returns to the reality of this God who both "sends" into the world and also "abides" in the fullness of his eternal life. The language in these chapters, as throughout the text, is both Trinitarian—the one God is expressed as a communion of Father, Son and Spirit—and missiological—sending and being sent are constitutive of the divine reality, and so normative for human reality also.

In the chapters framed by this theological account, *Generous Love* speaks successively of "Our contemporary context and our Anglican heritage" (2), and of the ways in which Anglican insights have been shaped by "Reading the scriptures" (3), and by "Tradition and reason" (4). It is made apparent in this part of the text that, while Anglicans rely on a distinctive theological method that rests on an understanding of God as Trinity, this is in no sense exclusive to Anglicanism, and indeed Anglican thinking in the whole area of inter-religious relations has been informed by a growing ecumenical consensus, flowing particularly from Vatican II's declaration *Nostra aetate*.

The document goes on to speak of three ways in which encounter with different faiths is leading Christians into a renewed experience of encounter with God: "Celebrating the presence of Christ's body" (5), "Communicating the energy of the Spirit" (6), and "Practising the embassy and hospitality of God" (7). While each of these reflects a particular dimension of the Church's presence and engagement in a religiously complex world, *Generous Love* also links each in turn with the Trinitarian logic that is at the heart of the Christian understanding of the One God and which runs through the whole text.

The character of *Generous Love* can be described as Trinitarian, missiological, and scriptural. The former two themes should be clear from what I have described above about the overall structure of the text. The use of scripture features in two ways: specifically and self-consciously, in chapter 3, titled "Shaping Anglican Insights: Reading the Scriptures"; but then also throughout the text in the way that biblical references and allusions are woven into the text of the argument. I shall look at each dimension in turn.

Reflections on Anglican Method

Chapter 3 of *Generous Love* addresses the way in which Anglican insights into interreligious questions are shaped by reading scripture. This account needs to be taken with the next chapter, dealing with tradition and reason, since the latter two are not independent routes to access theological truth; rather, they are means by which the riches embedded in the scriptures are to be uncovered and brought afresh to the attention of each generation. This Anglican teaching of the primacy of scripture—first formulated as a core principle of the Reformation—applies also to the role of experience in interpreting the Word: the people of God bring to their various contexts of today the normative texts canonized as Holy Scripture, and it is in a creative interaction with those diverse contexts that those texts speaks to them. The chapter then focuses on three aspects of this interaction.

The first is the way in which contemporary multireligious contexts can generate new readings of texts whose original contexts of inscription were themselves multireligious. This applies in the case of the Christian scriptures to both the Old and New Testaments, which were shaped for the situations of, respectively, Israel in the Ancient Near East, set among nations each following their own god, and the Apostolic Church in the Roman Empire and its neighboring states, particularly in cosmopolitan cities marked by a diversity of cults and philosophies. When Christians read these scriptures in multireligious contexts today, it argues, they find the texts coming to life as they are responding to challenges and opportunities already faced by the people of God in earlier contexts.

The document speaks second of the significance of the internal differentiation that marks the Christian Bible, where the Hebrew scriptures, known to Christians as the Old Testament, provide the context for the formation of the New Testament. In common with *Nostra aetate*, and drawing on the teaching of earlier Lambeth Conferences, it concludes from this that Christian-Jewish relations will always have for the church a particular significance within the wider world of interreligious relations.

Third, recognizing that in interreligious encounter the sacred scriptures of other religions can provide part of the context within which the biblical text is read, the chapter commends the practice of "Scriptural Reasoning," giving some examples of the way in which Christians can gain new insights from this. A

Scriptural Reasoning type-process has been at the heart of most of the Building Bridges seminars, and participants in these Christian-Muslim encounters have spoken of the way in which the attentive study together of biblical and Qur'ānic texts can open up a deep and honest dialogue in which the scriptures become a vehicle through which we encounter not only one another but God. However, it is important to realize that this does not require or imply that "scripture" is a univocal concept playing much the same role in different religions. In particular, Bible and Qur'ān are not seen in Christianity and Islam, respectively, as similarly conveying the Word of God; *Generous Love* makes it clear at the outset of this chapter that for Christians it is Jesus Christ who is the eternal Word of God, who is revealed through the words of Holy Scripture; amplifying this later, it describes how God "expresses himself in our midst in body language" (cap 5, §5).

The Use of the Bible

Besides the conscious reflections in chapter 3 on the reading of scriptural texts in context, the rest of *Generous Love* is itself a document marked by an extensive use of the Bible—twenty-four biblical citations are referenced in its notes, the overwhelming majority of them from the New Testament or the Psalms—which probably reflects a normal Anglican pattern. In addition to these citations, there are many other passages that allude to biblical passages, or that resonate with biblical imagery. In the main, it can be said that the use of the Bible in *Generous Love* is quite unself-conscious, and unmethodical, and in this it stands within a strong current of scriptural use in Christian literature, both Anglican and from other traditions. Through the Fathers and in particular through monastic writers, there developed a tradition of *ruminatio*, spending time to chew over the cud of the biblical texts through repeated reading, which resulted in a use of scriptural verses that could be quite free-ranging and unsystematic. This is the process referred to in one of the collects of the Book of Common Prayer, cited in *Generous Love*: "Blessed Lord, who hast caused all Holy Scriptures to be written for our learning: Grant that we may in such wise hear them, read, mark, learn, and inwardly digest them. . . ." This process results in an approach that has been described, using a phrase coined by Archbishop Rowan Williams, as "contemplative pragmatism."

However, this does not mean that scriptural verses can or should be simply selected in a manipulative way so as to reinforce a predetermined line of argument. While in a document like *Generous Love* the demands of brevity and clarity necessarily mean that texts are cited without their surrounding biblical contexts, they have not been chosen without regard for those contexts. Rather, the intention has been to shape an argument that faithfully reflects an authentic trajectory within the Bible's theological world, and to highlight, at various appropriate points in the document, texts that are illustrative of that trajectory. It is in this sense that *Generous Love* lays claim to being a "biblical" document: not that it is built on the foundation of a few verses used as premises for deductive reasoning, nor that it presents a compendium of scriptural teaching on interreligious issues, but that it seeks to map out a theological approach that is recognizably part of the biblical landscape, and in that mapping it highlights some passages and themes as key landmarks in the topography.

In practice, this happens in three ways. One is the citation of specific verses to encapsulate key elements of teaching. This is apparent in chapter 1, where a number of texts are given to express the nature of God in his engagement with the world: first, his universality (Ac 17), and then, successively, his generosity as Father (Ps 104, 1 Tim 2, Matt. 5), his revelation as Son (Heb 1, John 14, 2 Cor 4), and his energy as Spirit (Matt. 12, Gal 5). A second method engages with a larger unit of text, providing a summarizing paraphrase of an important episode in the Gospels. The example given in chapter 7 (§1) is that of the sending out by Jesus of seventy of his disciples (Luke 10); this is used to develop the theme of mission as embassy. A still wider scope is taken in the following paragraph, which refers to the images of hospitality found throughout the Bible. In terms of the analogy of biblical landscape that I suggested above, these three patterns of use could perhaps be likened, respectively, to a signpost standing in one place, to a map charting one journey, and to an overview of a whole territory. It will be for reader-travelers to judge how reliable and serviceable they are as navigation aids.

Generous Love and *A Common Word*

A Common Word strikes me, like *Generous Love*, as laying claim to being a deeply scriptural document. In both cases, this is not just a matter of political

expediency—because the Qur'ān or the Bible are one of the common posses-
sions of Muslims or Anglican Christians, and so provide a common vocabulary—but also reflects the way in which both texts are deeply imbued with
scriptural reference and allusion. This is not to say that the use of scripture in
both is the same; it is not. Most obviously, *A Common Word* cites the Bible as
well as the Qur'ān, while *Generous Love* restricts itself to Christian sources.
This reflects the differing backgrounds and audiences of the two documents.
Moreover, in *A Common Word*, some Qur'ānic verses are given especial promi-
nence as being in some sense foundational to the whole—notably 3.64, "Come
to a common word between us and you," from which the document takes its
name. However, in their different ways, both attest the centrality and primacy of
scripture for Muslims and Christians in the challenge of engaging with religious
difference, and both open up possibilities of scriptural dialogue.

These reflections on *Generous Love* and *A Common Word* prompt the following two questions for further consideration by those engaged in Christian-
Muslim dialogue:

1. How persuasive is our use of our own scripture to enable a generous
   response to each other?
2. What criteria will govern our use of each other's scripture in the process of
   inter-religious dialogue and to the end of inter-religious understanding?

Note

1. London: The Anglican Consultative Council, 2008. Reprinted by permission.

3.6   The Use of Scripture in *A Common Word*

REZA SHAH-KAZEMI

Reza Shah-Kazemi's essay is printed after the following text, which is the final section of *A Common Word*, "An Open Letter and Call from Muslim Religious Leaders" addressed to Christian leaders, dated October 13, 2007.[1]

(III) Come to a Common Word Between Us and You

A Common Word

Whilst Islam and Christianity are obviously different religions—and whilst there is no minimising some of their formal differences—it is clear that the *Two Greatest Commandments* are an area of common ground and a link between the Qur'an, the Torah and the New Testament. What prefaces the Two Commandments in the Torah and the New Testament, and what they arise out of, is the Unity of God—that there is only one God. For the *Shema* in the Torah, starts: (Deuteronomy 6:4) *Hear, O Israel: The LORD our God, the LORD is one!* Likewise, Jesus (PBUH) said: (Mark 12:29) *"The first of all the commandments is: 'Hear, O Israel, the LORD our God, the LORD is one"*. Likewise, God says in the Holy Qur'an: *Say: He, God, is One. / God, the Self-Sufficient Besought of all. (Al-Ikhlas, 112:1–2)*. Thus the Unity of God, love of Him, and love of the neighbour form a common ground upon which Islam and Christianity (and Judaism) are founded.

This could not be otherwise since Jesus (PBUH) said: (Matthew 22:40) *"On these two commandments hang all the Law and the Prophets."* Moreover, God confirms in the Holy Qur'an that the Prophet Muhammad (PBUH) brought nothing fundamentally or essentially new: *Naught is said to thee (Muhammad) but what already was said to the messengers before thee (Fussilat 41:43)*. And: *Say (Muhammad): I am no new thing among the messengers (of God), nor know I what will be done with me or with you. I do but follow that which is Revealed to me, and I am but a plain warner (Al-Ahqaf, 46:9).* Thus also God in the Holy Qur'an confirms that the same eternal truths of the Unity of God, of the necessity for total love and devotion to God (and thus shunning false gods), and of the necessity for love of fellow human beings (and thus justice), underlie all true religion:

> *And verily We have raised in every nation a messenger, (proclaiming): Worship God and shun false gods. Then some of them (there were) whom God guided, and some of them (there were) upon whom error had just hold. Do but travel in the land and see the nature of the consequence for the deniers! (Al-Nahl, 16:36)*
>
> *We verily sent Our messengers with clear proofs, and revealed with them the Scripture and the Balance, that mankind may stand forth in justice . . . (Al-Hadid, 57:25)*

Come to a Common Word!

In the Holy Qur'an, God Most High tells Muslims to issue the following call to Christians (and Jews—the *People of the Scripture*):

> *Say: O People of the Scripture! Come to a common word between us and you: that we shall worship none but God, and that we shall ascribe no partner unto Him, and that none of us shall take others for lords beside God. And if they turn away, then say: Bear witness that we are they who have surrendered (unto Him). (Aal 'Imran 3:64)*

Clearly, the blessed words: *we shall ascribe no partner unto Him* relate to the Unity of God. Clearly also, worshipping *none but God*, relates to being totally devoted to God and hence to the *First and Greatest Commandment*. According to one of the oldest and most authoritative commentaries (*tafsir*) on the Holy Qur'an—the *Jami' Al-Bayan fi Ta'wil Al-Qur'an* of Abu Ja'far Muhammad bin Jarir Al-Tabari (d. 310 A.H. / 923 C.E.)—*that none of us shall take others for lords beside God*, means 'that none of us should obey in disobedience to what God has commanded, nor glorify them by prostrating to them in the same way as they prostrate to God'. In other words, that Muslims, Christians and Jews should be free to each follow what God commanded them, and not have 'to prostrate before kings and the like'[21]; for God says elsewhere in the Holy Qur'an: *Let there be no compulsion in religion. . . . (Al-Baqarah, 2:256).* This clearly relates to the Second Commandment and to love of the neighbour of which justice[22] and freedom of religion are a crucial part. God says in the Holy Qur'an:

> *God forbiddeth you not those who warred not against you on account of religion and drove you not out from your homes, that ye should show them kindness and deal justly with them. Lo! God loveth the just dealers.* (Al-Mumtahinah, 60:8)

We thus as Muslims invite Christians to remember Jesus's (PBUH) words in the Gospel (Mark 12:29–31):

> *. . . the LORD our God, the LORD is one. / And you shall love the LORD your God with all your heart, with all your soul, with all your mind, and with all your strength.' This is the first commandment. / And the second, like it, is this: 'You shall love your neighbour as yourself.' There is no other commandment greater than these.*

As Muslims, we say to Christians that we are not against them and that Islam is not against them—so long as they do not wage war against Muslims on account of their religion, oppress them and drive them out of their homes, (in accordance with the verse of the Holy Qur'an [*Al-Mumtahinah*, 60:8] quoted above). Moreover, God says in the Holy Qur'an:

> *They are not all alike. Of the People of the Scripture there is a staunch community who recite the revelations of God in the night season, falling prostrate (before Him). / They believe in God and the Last Day, and enjoin right conduct and forbid indecency, and vie one with another in good works. These are of the righteous. / And whatever good they do, nothing will be rejected of them. God is Aware of those who ward off (evil).* (Aal-'Imran, 3:113–115)

Is Christianity necessarily against Muslims? In the Gospel Jesus Christ (PBUH) says:

> *He who is not with me is against me, and he who does not gather with me scatters abroad.* (Matthew 12:30)
> *For he who is not against us is on our side.* (Mark 9:40)
> *. . . for he who is not against us is on our side.* (Luke 9:50)

According to the *Blessed Theophylact's*[23] *Explanation of the New Testament*, these statements are not contradictions because the first statement (in the actual

Greek text of the New Testament) refers to demons, whereas the second and third statements refer to people who recognised Jesus, but were not Christians. Muslims recognize Jesus Christ as the Messiah, not in the same way Christians do (but Christians themselves anyway have never all agreed with each other on Jesus Christ's (PBUH) nature), but in the following way: . . . *the Messiah Jesus son of Mary is a Messenger of God and His Word which he cast unto Mary and a Spirit from Him* . . . (*Al-Nisa'*, 4:171). We therefore invite Christians to consider Muslims *not against* and thus *with them*, in accordance with Jesus Christ's (PBUH) words here.

Finally, as Muslims, and in obedience to the Holy Qur'an, we ask Christians to come together with us on the common essentials of our two religions . . . *that we shall worship none but God, and that we shall ascribe no partner unto Him, and that none of us shall take others for lords beside God* . . . (*Aal 'Imran*, 3:64).

Let this common ground be the basis of all future interfaith dialogue between us, for our common ground is that on which hangs *all the Law and the Prophets* (Matthew 22:40). God says in the Holy Qur'an:

> *Say (O Muslims): We believe in God and that which is revealed unto us and that which was revealed unto Abraham, and Ishmael, and Isaac, and Jacob, and the tribes, and that which Moses and Jesus received, and that which the prophets received from their Lord. We make no distinction between any of them, and unto Him we have surrendered. / And if they believe in the like of that which ye believe, then are they rightly guided. But if they turn away, then are they in schism, and God will suffice thee against them. He is the Hearer, the Knower. (Al-Baqarah, 2:136–137)*

Between Us and You

Finding common ground between Muslims and Christians is not simply a matter for polite ecumenical dialogue between selected religious leaders. Christianity and Islam are the largest and second largest religions in the world and in history. Christians and Muslims reportedly make up over a third and over a fifth of humanity, respectively. Together they make up more than 55 percent of the world's population, making the relationship between these two religious communities the most important factor in contributing to meaningful peace around the world. If Muslims and Christians are not at peace, the world cannot be at peace. With the terrible weaponry of the modern world; with Muslims and

Christians intertwined everywhere as never before, no side can unilaterally win a conflict between more than half of the world's inhabitants. Thus our common future is at stake. The very survival of the world itself is perhaps at stake.

And to those who nevertheless relish conflict and destruction for their own sake or reckon that ultimately they stand to gain through them, we say that our very eternal souls are all also at stake if we fail to sincerely make every effort to make peace and come together in harmony. God says in the Holy Qur'an: *Lo! God enjoineth justice and kindness, and giving to kinsfolk, and forbiddeth lewdness and abomination and wickedness. He exhorteth you in order that ye may take heed (Al Nahl, 16:90).* Jesus Christ (PBUH) said: *Blessed are the peacemakers. . . . .* (Matthew 5:9), and also: *For what profit is it to a man if he gains the whole world and loses his soul?* (Matthew 16:26).

So let our differences not cause hatred and strife between us. Let us vie with each other only in righteousness and good works. Let us respect each other, be fair, just and kind to another and live in sincere peace, harmony and mutual goodwill. God says in the Holy Qur'an:

> *And unto thee have We revealed the Scripture with the truth, confirming whatever Scripture was before it, and a watcher over it. So judge between them by that which God hath revealed, and follow not their desires away from the truth which hath come unto thee. For each We have appointed a law and a way. Had God willed He could have made you one community. But that He may try you by that which He hath given you (He hath made you as ye are). So vie one with another in good works. Unto God ye will all return, and He will then inform you of that wherein ye differ.* (Al-Ma'idah, 5:48)

Wal-Salaamu 'Alaykum,
Pax Vobiscum.

Notes on *A Common Word*

[21] Abu Ja'far Muhammad Bin Jarir Al-Tabari, *Jami' al-Bayan fi Ta'wil al-Qur'an, (Dar al-Kutub al-'Ilmiyyah,* Beirut, Lebanon, 1st ed, 1992/1412,) *tafsir* of Aal-'Imran, 3:64; Volume 3, pp. 299–302.

[22] According to grammarians cited by Tabari (op cit.) the word 'common' (*sawa'*) in 'a common word between us' also means 'just', 'fair' (*adl*).

[23] The Blessed Theophylact (1055–1108 C.E.) was the Orthodox Archbishop of Ochrid and Bulgaria (1090–1108 C.E.). His native language was the Greek of the New Testament. His *Commentary* is currently available in English from Chrysostom Press.

*   *   *

In this brief essay I offer some comments on the document titled *A Common Word*. In particular, I focus on the historical context, interpretation, and application of Qur'ān 3:64: "Say: 'O People of the Scripture! Come to a common word between us and you: that we shall worship none but God, and that we shall ascribe no partner unto Him, and that none of us shall take others for lords beside God.'"

This verse is the cornerstone of the document, and is applied in a manner that is clearly intended to point to the common ground upon which all members of the Abrahamic faiths stand together. It is interpreted as corresponding to the two "Supreme Commandments" of Jesus in the Bible, which are quoted in the document more than once, and the explicit claim is made that "the Unity of God, love of Him, and love of the neighbour form a common ground upon which Islam and Christianity (and Judaism) are founded."[2]

This appeal to the absolute values shared in common by the two faiths—and, implicitly, all faiths—has met with an extraordinary response, and appears to be a testimony to its timeliness and pertinence in the present religio-political climate. The document has, however, been regarded by certain critics as unexceptionable, if not platitudinous; others have argued that it smacks of reductionism: the religions are reduced to their lowest common denominator or a putative essence, à la John Hick, with all differences between the faiths being relegated to the periphery, and thus rendered both superfluous and inconvenient. From this arises the need, satisfied by John Hick, to refer to distinctive, traditionally held beliefs as "myths": just as Hick refers to "the Myth of God Incarnate," Muslim pluralists would be invited to return the compliment and affirm, for example, that the doctrine of the Qur'ān being the final Word of God is likewise a myth needing to be debunked.

There is another kind of criticism that would be leveled against the interpretation of the verse given here. At the Building Bridges seminar in Washington, DC, in 2004, three years before the launching of the Common Word initiative, Professor Mustansir Mir claimed that verse 3:64 comes in the context of "a serious indictment of the People of the Book." He notes that 3:61 directly refers to the *mubāhala*, an invitation by the Prophet to the visiting delegation of Christians of Najran to a mutual imprecation, an appeal to God to curse "the liars"—those who "lie," that is, about the nature of Jesus. The polemical tone of this passage implies, for Mir, that the invitation of verse 64, "Come to a common word," "is not an offer to find middle ground between Christianity and Islam," but rather "the phrase urges the claims of the Muslim interpretation of monotheism over against those of the Christian interpretation."[3]

Mir's remarks are in accord with the overall thrust of the exegetical tradition on this score. Most commentators do indeed read this verse in the light of the polemics that governed the historical event occasioning the revelation of the verse—the *sabab al-nuzūl*. However, there are some commentators who read the verse in a manner that is closer to that adopted in *A Common Word*; for example, Fakhr al-Din al-Razi regards the verse as an instruction to the Prophet to "leave the path of disputation" and opt for an alternative mode of engagement. Al-Razi says that the verse is in effect telling the Prophet to make an appeal to justice and fairness, an objective appeal to worship the One and only God, an appeal to which everyone of "sound intellect" will respond.[4] It might be argued that the authors of *A Common Word* go further than would be warranted even by this reading of 3:64, but al-Razi indicates a trajectory leading from polemics to dialogue, a trajectory that the authors of *A Common Word* have followed to what one might call a logical conclusion. The freshness and originality of the exegetical endeavor is also manifested by the creative use of biblical verses to uphold the basic argument.

What we see in *A Common Word* is an application of a duo-dimensional logic inherent in the Prophet's own mode of engagement with the Christians, a logic that is itself an application and reflection of the Qur'ānic discourse concerning the Other, as we hope to demonstrate in a moment. Whereas Professor Mir argues for a "post-prophetic theology of interfaith dialogue," the Common Word initiative demonstrates the perennial relevance of the prophetic mode of dialogue whereby difference is not ignored, but rather respected. The document makes no claim to go beyond the Prophet's paradigm in erecting a "post-prophetic" theology; rather, it expresses an attempt to be faithful to that paradigm, and invites us to consider its subtlety and polyvalence.

The subtlety of this paradigm can be observed by taking a closer look at the historical event with which this group of verses is associated, the visit of the Christian delegation of Najran to Medina in the ninth year after the Hijra (631). One especially significant aspect of this event is the fact that when the Christians requested to leave the city to perform their liturgy, the Prophet invited them to accomplish their rites in his own mosque.[5] According to Ibn Ishaq, who gives the standard account of this remarkable event—so little commented upon, alas—the Christians in question were "*Malikī*"; that is, Melchite, meaning that they followed the Byzantine Christian rites.[6] In other words, they enacted the Eucharistic rites that incorporated the fully developed trinitarianism of the orthodox councils, expressing the definitive creed of the divine sonship of Christ—doctrines robustly criticized in the Qur'ān. Nonetheless, the Prophet allowed the Christians to accomplish their rites in his own mosque. The most sacred spot for the Muslims in Medina was given over to the Christians for the enactment of rites embodying the doctrine of the divinity of Christ. We thus observe here a duo-dimensionality in the prophetic paradigm of interfaith engagement: theological denial on the plane of dogma coexists with spiritual affirmation on the superior plane of spiritual reality, that reality of which dogma is a limited, conceptual expression. Exoteric or theological distinction remains —and this is necessary for upholding the integrity of each path; while esoteric or spiritual identity is implied or intended. The summit is One, and the believer "tends toward" that oneness in sincere devotion, whatever be the form taken by that devotion.

The Prophet's words and his actions—his denials and his affirmations—must therefore be seen as a whole, the two dimensions complementing and not contradicting one another. The invitation to come to a "common word" is applied on both dimensions or levels: the "word" shared in common is the fundamental aspiration to worship the one and only God—the objective, transcendent, unique Reality. That which is not shared in common is the manner in which that Reality is conceived, and the mode by which that Reality is worshipped: fusion at the level of the essence, without any confusion at the level of forms. The dogmas and rituals of each faith are thus distinct and irreducible, while the summit of the path indicated by dogma and ritual is one and the same.

Here we have an application of the principle of interfaith dialogue explicitly called for by the Qur'ān: "Call unto the path of thy Lord with wisdom and fair exhortation; and hold discourse with them in that which is most excellent" (16:125). *Aḥsan*, here translated "most excellent," can also be translated as that which is most beautiful or most fine, the "common word" that expresses a shared devotion to the one and only reality, transcending all human categories, and that surely relates to that "most excellent" element in any discourse.

This duo-dimensional character of the Prophet's engagement with the Christians of Najran should thus be seen as a kind of commentary on the Qur'ānic discourse concerning the Other, taken as a whole, for this discourse likewise expresses two apparently contradictory dimensions. Salvation is promised to Christians (2:62; 5:69) and yet basic tenets of Christian theology are severely censured throughout the Qur'ān. Likewise, on the one hand, there is no essential difference between the messages brought by the prophets; and, on the other, God has revealed different rites, paths, and laws to different prophets for different communities. To take the first aspect: Muslims are told in the Qur'ān in various places not to "distinguish between" any of God's messengers. For example, as quoted in *A Common Word*: "Say: 'We believe in God and that which is revealed unto us, and that which was revealed unto Abraham and Ishmael and Isaac and Jacob and the tribes, and that which Moses and Jesus received, and that which the prophets received from their Lord. We make no distinction between any of them, and unto Him we have surrendered'" (2:136; almost identical at 3:84). On the other hand, emphasizing formal difference, we have this verse, also quoted in *A Common Word*: "For each We have appointed a Law and a Way. Had God willed, He could have made you one community. But that He may try you by that which He hath given you [He hath made you as you are]. So vie one with another in good works. Unto God ye will all return, and He will inform you of that wherein ye differed" (5:48). Thus, *A Common Word* cannot be accused of performing a Hickean reduction of religions to a common denominator that overlooks or ignores formal differences. It states: "Islam and Christianity are obviously different religions—and . . . there is no minimizing some of their formal differences. . . ." This respect for formal differences not only separates the document from any simplistic reductionism, it also stems from 5:48, which affirms that it is from the divine will and not human response (as Hick would have it) that different religions have arisen.

To return to the prophetic paradigm, we see the Prophet explicitly disagreeing with certain aspects of Christian dogma—to agree with them would be to abolish the distinction between the two religions, and thus subvert the divinely willed diversity, as well as contradict explicit Qur'ānic verses—but this explicit disagreement goes hand in hand with an implicit affirmation, an affirmation of the validity and hence efficacy of the rites embodying those dogmas. These rites are perceived, by the eye of the heart[7] and not through the prism of dogmatic theology, as modes of orientation toward the absolute Reality intended by faith as such, a Reality that infinitely transcends the relativities delineated both by conceptual belief and formal rites. In allowing the Christians to perform their

rites in his mosque, the Prophet was upholding the intended essence and ultimate source of those rites; he was not simply exercising a tactful tolerance of a
fundamentally flawed cult. This act can only be fully understood and appreci-
ated if one takes account of the fact that the universality and transcendence of
the essence intended by sincere devotion takes precedence over the particularities of its forms. To state baldly the message of *A Common Word*: That which
unites the believers is greater than that which divides them—infinitely greater,
one might say—for "Our God and your God is one God" (29:46).

It would not be out of place to conclude with this point, which is heavily
implied in *A Common Word*: it is this self-same God that is invoked in churches
and synagogues as well as in mosques. Thus we find that, when permission is
first given to Muslims to fight in self-defense, it was given explicitly for the sake
of protecting all such holy places and not just mosques: "Permission [to fight]
is given to those who are being fought, for they have been wronged, and surely
God is able to give them victory; those who have been expelled from their
homes unjustly, only because they said: Our Lord is God. Had God not driven
back some by means of others, monasteries, churches, synagogues and mosques
—wherein the name of God is oft-invoked—would assuredly have been destroyed" (22: 39–40).

Notes

1. For the full text of *A Common Word*, and further information, see www.acommon
word.com/. Reprinted here by permission.

2. For all citations of *A Common Word*, see the full text at www.acommonword.com/.
The document is not divided into pages or numbered paragraphs.

3. Mustansir Mir, "Scriptures in Dialogue: Are We Reckoning without the Host?" in
Michael Ipgrave, ed., *Bearing the Word: Prophecy in Biblical and Qur'ānic Perspective* (London: Church House, 2005), 15–16.

4. Fakhr al-Din al-Razi, *al-Tafsīr al-kabīr* (Beirut, 2001), vol. 3, 251.

5. Mir acknowledges this event but does not ascribe very much importance to it, referring
to it in terms of "hospitality" ("Scriptures in Dialogue," 16).

6. Ibn Ishaq, *The Life of Muhammad: A Translation of Ibn Ishaq's Sīrat Rasūl Allāh* (trans.
A. Guillaume; Oxford: Oxford University Press, 1968), 270–77.

7. *A Common Word* refers to the heart as the spiritual organ of perception. Mir also
refers to the "wholesome heart," without going much further ("Scriptures in Dialogue," 19).

Conversations in Rome

DAVID MARSHALL

This book consists chiefly of edited versions of papers delivered at the Building Bridges seminar in Rome in May 2008. But there was naturally much more to the seminar than these papers: above all, there was conversation, and plenty of it. There were a number of plenary sessions at which the papers were discussed or the proceedings of a whole day were mulled over. Rather more time, however, was given to discussion in groups of around seven whose membership remained the same throughout the seminar. These groups provided the context for conversations that started by engaging with the selected Christian and Islamic texts but often ranged much further afield.

The promotion of such conversation between Muslim and Christian scholars is a core aim of the Building Bridges project. Including some kind of record of the conversations at the Rome seminar is therefore highly desirable. The approach taken here is to give a relatively brief overview of the main themes that emerged in plenary and group discussions.[1] What is offered is not a heavily footnoted theological essay but rather an impression of a series of conversations in the course of which a wide range of views was expressed. There were differences both between Christian and Islamic perspectives and also between co-religionists; it should therefore not be assumed that any views recorded here were necessarily held by more than one participant. In line with "Chatham House Rules," the ideas expressed are unattributed.

This account of "Conversations in Rome" works with the same three broad themes around which the whole book is structured: revelation, translation, and interpretation. These themes of course frequently overlap with each other. A fourth area of discussion has been added to include some account of discussion of wider issues in dialogue between the faiths.

Revelation

Much discussion focused on what Christians and Muslims mean by speaking of scripture as revealed or inspired. The word-for-word revelation of the Qur'ān was contrasted with the inspiration of the Bible. Whereas in Islam the Prophet is not seen as fashioning the actual words of the revealed scripture, in Christianity the prophets are generally deemed to have put into their own words a message received through inspiration. For Christians, the idea of prophets or other scriptural authors being inspired by God has generally had one of two meanings: the older view was that it was only when writing that they were inspired; the more recent view has been that their life as a whole was the locus of inspiration. In Islamic theology, whether the Qur'ān was considered created (the Mu'tazilite thesis) or uncreated (the Ash'arite thesis), Muslim theologians always considered the revelation to be the exact speech (*kalām*) of God.

The question was asked: How can a transcendent God speak in a created language without being diminished in status? One modern Muslim response is to assert that the Prophet received inspiration (as in the Christian perspective) and put this into his own words. According to Fazlur Rahman (1919–88), the Qur'ān is both the Word of God and, at the same time, the word of the Prophet.[2] This position was strongly criticized. Rahman appears to have felt it necessary to ascribe the authorship of the Qur'ān, at least partly, to the Prophet out of a perceived need to safeguard divine transcendence. God in his utter transcendence could not enter into human language without detriment to his transcendence; hence, the authorship of the actual words of the Qur'ān must be ascribed to the human being, the Prophet, even while accepting the fact that he received the spirit of the revelation, unarticulated, through the angel Gabriel. Against this position it was argued that one can, at one and the same time, uphold the transcendence of God and the sole authorship of the Qur'ān by God by recourse to the principle of immanence. Just as God's transcendence above all things is not compromised by his immanence within them, so the transcendent divinity can be the sole author of the Qur'ān. The divine presence within the scripture, and as the scripture, represents the aspect of divine immanence, which complements the aspect of divine transcendence. The classical dilemma regarding the Qur'ān was that it was either a human fabrication or else revealed by God. There was no third possibility: it could not be seen as both human and divine.

The question was asked whether belief in the Qur'ān as the final revelation implied that inspiration was ruled out subsequent to the Qur'ān. In response, reference was made to Ibn 'Arabi (1165–1240), who claimed that every word of his magnum opus, *al-Futūḥāt al-makkiyya*, was written under direct divine inspiration; and that his most commented upon work, *Fuṣūṣ al-ḥikam*, was given to him in a vision by the Prophet. However, Ibn 'Arabi would not have regarded these "inspirations" as "revelation" in the strict sense—the latter, *tanzīl*, is granted only to prophets, and the Qur'ān would be seen by Ibn 'Arabi, in line with Islamic orthodoxy, as being the final "revelation."

It was argued that the idea of the Bible as the Word of God was of post-Reformation origin; prior to this, the Word of God was seen as Christ only, with the scriptures seen as oracles of God. It was suggested that this shift in emphasis from Christ as the sole Word of God to the Bible also constituting the Word of God might well have been partly influenced by the Islamic perspective. Just as post-Reformation Christians came to adopt something akin to the Islamic conception of the revealed Book constituting the divine Word, so certain modern Muslims seem to have arrived at their conception of the scripture as being coauthored by God and the Prophet. Perhaps there has been a degree of reciprocal influence.

Christians have generally not had a problem in recognizing certain stylistic weaknesses in the Bible. These can even be seen as deliberate: they are intended to direct the reader to look through the style to the substance. Christians can accept without embarrassment the *sermo humilis*, or humble speech, of scripture, believing that this human modesty points inversely to the majesty of the divine substance. The intention behind the stylistic shortcomings has indeed been interpreted as a device to force Christians to focus on what is perfect and flawless: the Word of God made flesh in Jesus. At this point, the contrast with Islam is very clear as the Qur'ān is deemed to be the perfect and flawless manifestation of the divine, both in style and substance, conceptual meaning and spiritual presence. The inimitability (*i'jāz*) of the Qur'ān was discussed here, together with its implications for the development of local dialects, which were enriched, and not impoverished, by the central sacramental role played by Qur'ānic Arabic. One observes a multiplicity of languages and cultures operating within a unity determined by the Arabic of the Qur'ān. In modern times, the decline in reverence for the Qur'ān as the Word of God has weakened the foundations of Islamic unity.

It was noted that while both scriptures contain a mixture of genres, some occurring in both (such as narrative and legal material), an essential difference is that in the Bible God appears as a "character" in ways that are not found in the Qur'ān. Another significant difference is the tendency in Islam (but not in Christianity) to make clear distinctions between various degrees and modes of inspiration and revelation.

The point is often made in Christian-Muslim dialogue that the centrality of the Qur'ān in Islam corresponds to the centrality in Christianity not of the Bible but of Jesus Christ, the Word made flesh. However, not all Christians approach this point in quite the same way; those holding a doctrine of biblical inerrancy have a view of scriptural revelation that may have some affinity with that held by Muslims. This area of dialogue, with its concern to identify the most apt points of correspondence between the two faiths, was pursued further, in particular through comparison of the Qur'ān and the Eucharist. For all the obvious differences between the two, there is a suggestive analogy to explore between the ways that "Real Presence" is conveyed by the "elements" of the Arabic language, on the one hand, and bread and wine, on the other. Furthermore, traditionally it is not possible for alternatives to "translate" the presence conveyed solely by these appointed elements.

There was some discussion of how Islamic understandings of revelation strike Christians, to whom it seems much more natural that the God who made human beings "in his own image" would choose to be revealed through a human being rather than through a book. The perfect human being is surely much more fully representative of the plenitude of divine reality than any book could be. To this, a Muslim might respond that it is precisely because human beings are made in the image of God (as a ḥadīth teaches) that there arises the risk of idolatry (*shirk*): the worshipping of the human being in place of God. Thus, hearing, rather than seeing, the divine Word is the most appropriate way of relating to God, for the apparently more abstract mode of reception ensures that the divine transcendence is not compromised by a too-easy human mode of perception. From within the Christian tradition, one might note here the teaching of Meister Eckhart (1260–1327), for whom even the image of Christ can be a hindrance, if it is the pure unity of God that one wishes to realize. For Eckhart, silent stillness, with no images whatsoever, is best of all for the contemplative; it is a state that cannot be exchanged with any other without losing something essential.

At a practical level, it was suggested that, especially in view of all the difficulties in understanding one another's scriptures, the cause of Muslim-Christian dialogue would be well served by a new kind of scriptural commentary. Such "cross boundary" commentaries would assume less background knowledge than is usually the case and would seek to make scriptures more accessible to those of other faiths.

Translation

The comparison already noted between the Qur'ān and the Eucharist was pursued further in relation to the untranslatability of the Qur'ān. It was argued that while the doctrinal content of the Qur'ān is susceptible to translation, its theurgic power—its capacity to make God present—is untranslatable. This is why Muslims maintain the strict untranslatability of the Qur'ān, for the result of any translation, however useful at one level, will be sacramentally inefficacious. This helps to explain the reason why the Arabic language is so deeply venerated throughout the Muslim world. It was also pointed out that the Islamic spiritual practice of *dhikr Allāh* ("remembrance of God") is only performed using the Arabic (Qur'ānic) names of God. Thus the vocabulary of a specific Arabic dialect came to assume a metaphysical status, acquiring not just a transcendent status, but also imparting a powerful unifying force. Throughout the length and breadth of the Muslim world, all rites, rituals, and remembrance continue to be articulated through the Arabic of the Qur'ān.

An alternative Muslim viewpoint placed the emphasis rather differently. It was argued that neither the Qur'ān nor the sayings of Muhammad imply that the Qur'ān is in any sense a better or more civilized language than any other. Translations of the Qur'ān are essential, even taking into account the hazards that accompany them. Some of the difficulties in this area arise from the fact that translations have had a range of different underlying motivations, sometimes more political and cultural than religious.

It was recognized that the different instincts within the two faiths in relation to translation, together with the different practices that Christians and Muslims have developed, arise from their contrasting fundamental premises about the revelation of the divine Word in flesh and as book. The fact that it can be difficult, especially at a popular level, to grasp the perspectives of the other faith in this area with sympathetic understanding underlines the need for further careful dialogue.

Interpretation

Within both Christianity and Islam there are extensive and sophisticated traditions of reflection on how scripture is to be interpreted. Thomas Aquinas (1225–74), for example, in line with medieval traditions of exegesis, which in turn built on patristic approaches, taught that there is a hierarchy of levels of meaning in the Bible: literal, allegorical, moral, and anagogical. He emphasized that the literal sense is where we must start. This concerns the intention of scripture and should not be confused with "literalism." When the Bible speaks of God's arm, for example, the "literal" meaning is not a physical limb but rather God's purpose. Comparisons were drawn with Islamic writing on the multiple meanings of the Qur'ān; it was suggested that Sufi approaches to interpretation resemble the allegorical tendencies of the Alexandrian school more than the Antiochene emphasis on literal meaning. It has been an interesting recent development in Christian hermeneutics that the postmodern climate has encouraged the rediscovery of a wide range of types of interpretation, including allegory.

The need to understand the original context of passages of scripture is a major concern of the classical Islamic exegetical tradition. The asbāb al-nuzūl literature, which specifies the "causes" or "occasions" of the revelation of particular Qur'ānic passages, was produced for this purpose. Here reference was again made to Fazlur Rahman, who argued that contemporary Islamic hermeneutics needs to determine the meaning of the Qur'ān in its original context in order to apply the underlying scriptural message to the new context of the modern world.[3] It was suggested that this was a way of respecting the tradition without being locked in the past, a modernist approach that does not saw off the branch on which one is sitting.

A major topic of conversation was how religious traditions conceive of change from one period of revelation to another. Within Christianity, what are the strengths and weaknesses of the idea of "progressive revelation"? It was suggested that this notion can lead Christians to ignore the Old Testament or be dismissive of it. It is a sad fact that Christians still tend to regard the survival of the Jews as an unfortunate accident; Jews are somehow "failed Christians." This perspective may not be articulated consciously but can be seen, for example, in how lectionaries sometimes juxtapose passages from the Old and New Testaments, implying a transition from an era of harshness to one of mercy.

With the coming of Christ the Mosaic law was not so much abrogated as consummated or perfected (Matthew 5:17); there are links here with the claim elsewhere in the New Testament that it was God's purpose that "apart from us" the heroes of Israelite faith "would not be made perfect" (Hebrews 11:40). A connection could also be made here with traditional teaching on the Patriarchs awaiting Christ for their liberation from Limbo. Furthermore, Jesus says, referring to himself, "something greater than the temple is here" (Matthew 12:6). The material temple is replaced by the presence of Jesus. All the laws of purity associated with the temple were of course "superseded" inasmuch as the Temple itself ceased to exist in 70 CE. By the time the Gospel of Matthew was written, after the destruction of the second temple, all Jews had to rethink the meaning of the laws that were so integrally tied up with temple rituals.

In Christian perspective, the law was fulfilled in spirit, resulting in an overflow of concern from the domain of the law *per se* to the more profound domain of the principles that underlie the law. Thus, in the case of the adulteress (John 8:1–11), Jesus turns attention away from the outward accomplishment of the penalty to the question of intrinsic justice: Who could act justly in stoning the adulteress? The very presence of Jesus transforms, rather than abrogates, the law. When he says to the woman "neither do I condemn thee, go and sin no more," he confirms the spirit underlying the law and points to the purpose of the law—putting things right, rather than just punishing transgression. It was noted that there is a parallel to this in the Qur'ān that accepts the legal logic of the "eye for an eye" principle, but adds that if one can forego the right to retaliation this will be deemed an expiation for one's own shortcomings (5:45).

The concept of abrogation (*naskh*) has been highly significant within Islam, in terms both of the interpretation of different passages of the Qur'ān in relation to each other and also of the relationship of Islam as a whole to earlier religious traditions. Those Muslim scholars who accept the principle of abrogation within the Qur'ān—not all in fact do so—generally agree that it applies only to passages concerned with legal matters. It can thus be claimed that, since there are only some 600 Qur'ānic verses that can be classified as "legal," the whole question of abrogation has little bearing on the overwhelming thrust of the Qur'ānic message, which is fundamentally theological, ethical, spiritual, cosmological, and teleological.

It was asked whether the authority of the Qur'ān is undermined by the notion of some of its verses being abrogated by others. Does abrogation imply that the Qur'ān contradicts itself? It was argued that, on the contrary, abrogation further reinforces the authority of the Qur'ān, for it implies that the Qur'ān needs no external authority by means of which it is to be adjusted in order to respond to changing circumstances. The underlying logic of abrogation is that when circumstances changed, the Qur'ānic rulings adapted to those changes. This also indicates a methodology to be pursued by those who take the Qur'ān as a source of law: to be prepared to adapt to changing circumstances using the Qur'ānic mode of adjustment as a paradigm. Hence, even in extending the domain of the law to cover circumstances not explicitly dealt with by the Qur'ān, one is applying a Qur'ānic rather than an extra- or non-Qur'ānic principle. This point is made by Allama Hilli (1250–1325) in his commentary on *Tajrīd al-i'tiqād* of Nasir al-Din Tusi (1201–74): *naskh* became necessary because of hundreds of years elapsing since the previous dispensation. The implications for today are that Muslims need to engage in *ijtihād*, creative reinterpretation.

The principle of *naskh* is also applied to the abrogation by the Islamic Sharī'a of previous revealed legal dispensations, though the ethical norms and spiritual principles of the previous revelations are not subject to abrogation, given that all messengers sent by God were given the selfsame message. However, it was also noted that the question of abrogation takes on a more theological character when the legal codes of previous religious traditions are deemed to be abrogated by Islam. More widely, to speak of law is, inescapably, to speak of theology. How human beings obey God is an intrinsic aspect of their relationship to God; how society is ruled is similarly a theological as much as a legal or social issue. The question of abrogation thus has huge implications for individuals and society alike.

It was recognized that in both Christianity and Islam most believers understand the claim to finality made by their faith as implying the supersession and consequent superfluity of Judaism, in the case of Christianity, and of both Judaism and Christianity, in the case of Islam. There are, however, many different approaches to this question. Ibn 'Arabi, for example, had an ingenious way of applying the doctrine of *naskh*. He taught that Islam's abrogation of previous religions was like the sunrise in relation to the stars. The lights of the stars, far from being extinguished by the sun, have the light of the sun added to their own lights, so that the truth of these religions are rendered more luminous, more fully "realized," and not rendered null and void. Only "the ignorant," he said, believe that the pre-Qur'ānic religions are rendered null and void by abrogation.

Another major focus of discussion was the possibility of consensus in interpretation, over against a strong tendency toward fragmentation encouraged, especially in the West, by the forces of individualism and postmodernism. In relation to consensus (*ijmā'*) among Muslims, two different perspectives emerged. On the one hand, while it was acknowledged that Islam has no formal magisterium, it was argued that there had been significant recent examples of the *ijmā'* of orthodox scholars from all legal traditions, notably *A Common Word* and the Amman Message, which were regarded as authoritative statements against illegitimate and anarchic interpretations of Islam.[4] On the other hand, it was argued that, however laudable these initiatives might be, uniformity in interpretation cannot be enforced across the Muslim world, which consists of multitudes of communities producing interpretations relevant to their own contexts and serving their own needs. There are many current debates among Muslims from which no real consensus is emerging. Perhaps Muslims today lack the conceptual sophistication of the classical tradition that would be necessary to address the issues effectively. Meanwhile, there are many charismatic young Muslims "issuing fatwās left and right." "Can you control that? No, you can't."

An interesting discussion touched on the "illusion of continuity" that sometimes has to be maintained when religious communities are negotiating a difficult transition from one interpretation of their tradition to another. It was suggested that in order for Muslims to move forward certain parts of their tradition (regarding slavery, for example) sometimes needed to be "conveniently ignored" rather than addressed directly. It was recognized, with good humor, that the illusion of continuity was not unknown within Christianity.

Somewhat related to the theme of consensus, there was some discussion of the balance in both traditions between the place of the individual and the community. On the one hand, there are strong impulses, in Christianity and Islam alike, drawing individuals into identification with the larger whole to which they belong. For Muslims, the Hajj and the communal fast in Ramadan are just two of the more obvious practices deepening the individual's sense of belonging to the wider community. Tertullian (c. 160–c. 220) said that one Christian is no Christian and an ancient Eucharistic prayer contains the words: "Even as this broken bread was scattered over the hills, and was gathered together and became one, so let Your Church be gathered together from the ends of the earth into Your kingdom" (*Didache* ix,4). On the other hand, both traditions also recognize the individual dimension of faith. The social function of the mosque is important but, with no priest officiating or mediating, each individual prays for himself, even if standing behind an imam. Within Christianity there has always been a role for hermits, who, despite being apart from society, function as models of the religious life, indicating for all a spiritual trajectory that should be respected if not followed.

Relationships and Dialogue between the Faiths

The question was asked: What does it mean to say that we engage in dialogue out of love for the other? How can we love the unknown, the stranger? Is this not the most challenging test of our willingness to enter into dialogue, to do so on the basis of an affirmation of our love of the stranger, before we even know him or her? This may be the ideal, to love before we enter into dialogue, but a more realistic approach, perhaps, is to say that while we aim to love the stranger as an outcome of dialogue, the initial motivation for dialogue is hospitality. In putting forth a more nuanced version of this position, it was stressed that we should retain love as the principle of dialogue, but define love in this context as a fundamental disposition and not just as a sentiment. Hospitality and courtesy can be seen as stemming from this fundamental loving disposition, which can then develop into a deeper love based on increased knowledge of the other.

There was some discussion of the theological sources of the notion of "Generous Love."[5] The importance of St. John's Gospel was stressed, as this contains the seeds of a theology of the inherent mutuality of love. Love is of the very essence of the divine nature, so human beings, created as they are in the divine image, reflect divine love in their love for each other, however imperfectly. Jesus's words "Lend, hoping for nothing in return" (Luke 6:35) speak of the necessity of selflessness in love. Ultimately, love must transcend all natural ties, such as to one's family and even to one's own ego. What could be more different from God than the creation? So if God loves the creation—the relative, finite, imperfect world, so utterly different from his absoluteness, infinity, and perfection—and if God's love is the ultimate model of love, then surely we must love those strangers whom we know least, who may be utterly alien to us in some respects, and love them with a divine love, transcending all our own natural ties to self, family, nation, and religion. This is the test of our love, the extent to which we can love the utterly other, and thus reflect the love that God has for the whole of the creation.

Muslim participants related the Islamic conception of love to the principle of *rahma* (mercy, compassion), noting that this word is derived from *rahim* (womb) and so conveys the idea of the whole of creation being encompassed by the divine loving compassion. But it was also observed that in Islam love is subordinated to law and that, in relation to God's acts, there appears to be a very different conception of God in the two religions, even if the God believed in is one and the same.

A Christian participant commented that the impression made by reading the Qur'ān was that it was "all about God." The closer believers from different religions come to a conception of the ultimate, ineffable reality, the closer they come to overcoming their differences. For example, despite the vast differences in the metaphysical beliefs of Buddhists and Christians, the experience of shared meditative silence can bring both to feel that they are embraced by the same ineffable reality, a reality in which their differences dissolve. This does not mean that one's own tradition has been "left behind," but that one has experienced something that could not be expressed in words or acts, "a space which is neither mine nor yours," and that contains us all.

The importance of studying history as a key way to overcome stereotypes was affirmed. It can help us develop a critical view of our own tradition and a willingness to recognize all that has been good in the history of other traditions. What we now know about history bestows upon us all a moral responsibility; we must impart this knowledge to others in order to dispel myths and stereotypes about the other. The same principle applies to the study of the religious thought of the other tradition. The ignorance about the other's faith displayed by both Christians and Muslims may have been understandable in the past but is no longer excusable today. Careful and sympathetic study of each other's doctrines should be a high priority for all committed to Christian-Muslim dialogue.

Notes

1. This chapter draws on recordings of plenary sessions and on notes made by participants in some, but not all, of the small groups. No claim is made that this is a comprehensive account. Particular thanks are due to Reza Shah-Kazemi for the extensive notes that he provided.

2. Fazlur Rahman, *Islam*, 2nd ed. (Chicago: University of Chicago Press, 1979), ch. 2.

3. Fazlur Rahman, *Islam and Modernity: Transformation of an Intellectual Tradition* (Chicago: University of Chicago Press, 1982).

4. On *A Common Word*, see Reza Shah-Kazemi's chapter in this volume. On the Amman Message, see www.ammanmessage.com/.

5. See Michael Ipgrave's chapter in this volume on the Anglican document, *Generous Love*.

Afterword

ROWAN WILLIAMS

Islam, Christianity, and Judaism share a commitment to testing their claims and practice in the light of a sacred text believed to be inspired by God. While other faiths have sacred books, the Abrahamic faiths are distinct in looking to a single narrative that unifies the texts they study. But that apparently simple correlation proves to be a lot more complex when examined closely. For Christians, even the most resolutely fundamentalist, the text is a *witness* to the action of God, not itself the primary act of God (though its composition is directly under the direction of God). For the Muslim, the dictation of the Qur'ān is the normative divine action—the way in which God provides an authoritative touchstone for assessing any other narrative or prophecy or teaching, any other claim to "revealed truth." It is emphatically not the sole source of revelation, which, in Islam, is of course a continuous flow of divine teaching from the time of Adam onward; but it is the definitive criterion for understanding this stream of communication.

This has led some to say that the Qur'ān for the Muslim holds a place more like that of the incarnate Logos in Christianity than that of the Bible. But this, too, is less straightforward when examined, as many chapters in this volume make plain. Whatever the speculations in some Islamic traditions about the preexistence in heaven of the Qur'ān (comparable to claims made for the Torah in Rabbinic Judaism), it would be quite misleading to think of a sort of "incarnation" in the form of a book. The Qur'ān is something spoken and then obediently recited, an *event* in which God sets the boundaries of true teaching so that when the human voice echoes the divine voice of the Qur'ān, truth is made definitively present. But this is not the same as some sort of oracular approach in which the text instantly answers all specific questions. God is active in the form of the words spoken and received. But that activity still has to be understood and applied. Even if this is primarily—as it has often been in Islamic

175

history—a matter of precise linguistic analysis without what a Western intellect might regard as contextual interpretation, it remains a task to be performed, something to be filled out in the contingencies of human behavior and interaction. It is not the case that the Qur'ān as holy *object* is somehow a parallel to the historical flesh of Jesus Christ.

In Christianity, the fact that both Christ and the scriptures have been called the "Word" of God has sometimes made for confusion, especially among those who do not realize that the biblical use of "Word" reflects a far more nuanced term in Greek. For classical Christian theology, in the patristic period and the early Middle Ages, God's first self-communication is the second person of the Trinity, the divine intelligence itself existing eternally as a presence in relation to the divine source. What scripture does is to narrate the story of how human beings are summoned into relation with this divine relationship, that of Father and Son; and because they are summoned and enabled by nothing less than God, Christians speak of the eternal Holy Spirit as the agency by which we are incorporated into Christ's relation with the Father. Since scripture is a primary vehicle for our being formed in the likeness of Christ, it is seen as the Spirit's work; it is shaped by the Spirit, "breathed by God" in a well-known New Testament phrase (2 Timothy 3:16). It is "the Word written," as the Christian Reformers liked to express it, in the sense that it is definitively what God wants us to know securely about his nature and his actions. For most of Christian history and by most Christian believers, it has been regarded as infallible or inerrant in what it teaches about God—and frequently inerrant about everything else as well, including historical facts, though this last is not a claim many Western theologians would defend these days.

The difference between the two accounts, Muslim and Christian, of the character of the sacred text is thus something like this. The Christian sees scripture as one essential vehicle for being brought into conformity with the life of the Incarnate Word or Mind or Life-Pattern of God (*logos* in Greek), so as to grow in relation through him with the Father. The Muslim sees the Qur'ān as the core of divine communication, the text that spells out the essential nature and content of submission to God's will. But the difference does not mean that comparable issues do not arise. Any text has to be *read*, and any reading will in some way constitute an interpretation. What is more, both Christian and Islamic scripture are already *reinterpretations* of an earlier set of texts, and in some degree an interpretative commentary on those texts. They tell us straight away that holy texts can have a history, that they are read repeatedly and may only become clear when placed in a radically new light. Prophecy is fulfilled; corruptions or obscurities are cleared away. This does not imply that the existing text is in any way provisional or that we do not really know what it means. But it does gently remind us that the text is itself an active moment of reimagining the past.

And the Muslim insistence—from a very early period in Islamic history—that there is something irreplaceable about the medium of the Arabic language represents in part a recognition that translation is an interpretative exercise, and that the "territory" within which interpretation has to be exercised may need to be limited. Christianity has assumed, again from very early on, and with some important theological implications, that scripture can be and has to be translated; but this has led to questions about the authority of this or that translation, and it would be misleading to say that the church was essentially more relaxed about interpretative pluralism than Islam. So despite the significant and interesting divergences, neither faith escapes questions around the limits of legitimate interpretation.

Texts have to be read. And it is important to realize that this has meant, for most of Christian and Muslim history, "read publicly or corporately." Early Christians and early Muslims would not have thought of books as we do—commodities readily available and widely possessed. Hardly any early or mediaeval Christians would or could have owned "a Bible." Even clergy would know the text through liturgical books, with the readings prescribed for particular events. And the Qur'ānic text would have been assimilated by oral learning for most of the faithful. This point is worth pondering, simply because of the dangers of removing either text from its actual *use*. A facile opposition between Christianity as focused on a person and Islam as focused on a book usually presupposes a modern sense of what a book is, as opposed to the highly personal associations of something that is *recited*. Christianity looks toward a realized and deepened relation with the person spoken of in its text, primarily with God as revealed in Jesus. But Islam hears the Qur'ān as a direct spoken invitation to obedience, justice, and service rather than regarding it as the sort of text we are familiar with as moderns, an object that can be taken up and discarded at will or as a "code" abstracted from relationships.

Words generate other words. Even what appears to be repetition carries subtle change, as often as not, even if it is simply in an awareness of a new context for a reading. And one aspect of this generation of new words is that the meanings that are sensed in the text are likely to be expanding as time goes on, and may even be seen as in tension with the immediate surface meaning of the original words. In Christianity, this has produced a rich, if often problematic, legacy of symbolic interpretation—and a counter-move toward a supposed "literal" meaning as determinative (often on the assumption that the surface meaning is more likely to reflect authorial intention, divine and/or human). Augustine in the fifth and Thomas Aquinas in the thirteenth century are careful to warn against any idea that "literal" always equals a "plain" meaning. The sense of the letter is the sense of the text's purpose and genre, and we should be wary of thinking that the primary sense was some kind of simple pictorial reference (talking about the arm of the Lord does not mean that God has physical limbs). In some contexts, Christians are called on to clarify this principle in dialogue with Muslims, to avoid misreadings and misrepresentations. But Muslims, too, have rules of thumb for reading that Christians should be aware of, lest they fall into the common trap of lifting isolated passages out of the Qur'ān and judging Islam by them.

However difficult it is to give a tidy theological account of it, interpretation is unavoidable in both traditions. And many of the chapters in this book will underline, even if implicitly, the point that it is more constructive to *acknowledge* a history of interpretation than otherwise. Failure to do this leads to those varieties of primitivism that recur in Christian and Muslim history—"back to the unadorned text!"—and have the effect of privileging interpretations that have no accountability and no sense of being the result of *corporate* reading. The modern believer is not the first reader of the text; s/he reads something that has already been read and digested and interpreted in life as well as in thought, in ways that have almost certainly influenced the present act of individual reading or hearing. This is why it is important for both Christians and Muslims to be clear that modern fundamentalisms (not that the term is really helpful in the Islamic context) are indeed radically modern strategies, opposed to the ethos of tradition and community and to the whole basic recognition that the holy text is a divine *act* that is received in company with others scattered in both time and space, and so cannot be reduced to a piece of lucid impersonal information. In different ways, both faiths see the reading/reciting/hearing of the holy text as inseparable from growth in holiness, growth as a member of the community that God calls.

Perhaps, though, one of the most important themes to emerge from all the diverse discussions recorded here is that if we have a faith that insists on our attention to the performing or reciting of a holy text, we have to learn how to listen. Although none of the contributions here refers explicitly to the disciplines of silence in religious practice, this is clearly a dimension of how we are to absorb holy words, however exactly we understand them. When the Qur'ān is recited, when the gospel is read in the Christian Eucharist or the psalms sung in the monastic office, what is happening for the believer or practitioner is not an exercise in passing on helpful information, nor even in providing words that helpfully save us the trouble of thinking for ourselves how to speak of God or to God. It is an event in which God is believed to be active. For that action to impinge upon us in ways that transform us, we need to learn the appropriate receptivity; and that is what brings us to silence. It may be the literal silence of waiting for the words to be spoken to us, or the inner silence of stripping away our expectations so that, in the resonant image of a great Christian mystic, the Word may be born in us.

Islam and Christianity alike give a high valuation to the conviction that God speaks to us. Grasping what that does and does not mean, avoiding the crudity of thinking of scripture as an oracle, is challenging theological work, but at least it makes us think of our reading and listening as potentially an event in which God acts, and so too an event in which we are invited closer to God. The method used in the Building Bridges seminars has normally been one in which careful attention to each other's scriptures has been central. One of the insights of the exercise has been summed up as the attempt to "look at each others' faces as they are when turned toward God"—or, as we might say in the light of this reflection, as they look when they are listening expectantly for God to speak. By God's grace, there have been many moments in the seminars when the sense of listening to another's listening has been movingly palpable. I hope that these essays will offer some such moments to many more beyond the compass of our conversations at the Palazzola in 2008.

Index